NEW DIRECTIONS IN JEWELLERY II

LIN CHEUNG
BECCY CLARKE
INDIGO CLARKE

NEW DIRECTIONS IN JEWELLERY II

black dog
publishing

amy sackville

INTRODUCTION

This second volume of *New Directions in Jewellery* expands the territory set out in the first, offering a fascinating insight into some of the most innovative practices in jewellery design today. From established makers like Karl Fritsch, Ted Noten and Monika Brugger, to exciting emerging talents like Madeleine Furness and Carla Nuis, the works shown here, each in their own way, test the techniques and concepts of the medium. As this collection shows, the contemporary jewellery scene is thriving as never before, and a loose network of makers, teachers, galleries and institutions is pushing in ever more interesting and diverse new directions.

What becomes apparent in exploring and enjoying these pieces is the level of personal involvement that each jeweller feels in relation to their work. Whether highly conceptual or primarily formal in intent, the jewellery shown here is typified by an intelligent, informed and at times emotional engagement with the medium. Individual pieces of jewellery, however, like any artwork, have always been invested with meaning above and beyond the intention of the maker, and it is this idea that Lin Cheung's essay, "Wear, wearing, worn: The transitions of jewels to jewellery", addresses. With a sensitivity that is apparent in her own work, also shown within these pages, Cheung sets out the notion of what she calls 'jewellery-to-be', arguing that no jewel is complete until it is worn. She examines the work of makers, a number of whom are featured here, who specifically engage with this notion, from Dinie Besems' *Chalk Chain*, which leaves marks upon the clothing of the wearer, to Mah Rana's ongoing project *Meanings and Attachments*. In conclusion, Cheung presents a new way of thinking about, making, and wearing jewellery, a "new jewellery utopia" which will lead us to "a greater understanding of the personal and social values made manifest through all objects".

The remainder of the book is divided into loose groupings; as in the first volume, this is intended less as a strict system of classification than as a means of negotiating what is an inevitably wide and varied selection. The reader is invited to make associations not only within the given categories, but across the book as a whole, in considering how jewellery functions today on every level from the personal to the political; in doing so, Cheung's manifesto perhaps provides an underlying point of reference. To facilitate this way of thinking, selected makers have been afforded more space to examine the broader issues that their work raises; from the use of humour, to the relationship between jewellery and the body, to the ways in which jewellery is both knit up in, and can comment upon, social conditions.

While jewellery is perhaps most commonly associated with artifice and immaculate form – from the perfect, simple circle to elaborate cutting, shaping and layering – the makers shown in the first chapter, "Natural Selection", turn to the natural world as a source of inspiration and, at times, material. The process behind these works is no less complex or skilled, but the result is pieces that take on something of the precepts of nature. It is this point of departure that unites the varied practices profiled here. These jewelleries incorporate or imitate botanic specimens, hair, sponges, wood, shells. Some, like that of Julie Blyfield, are carefully crafted replicas of natural forms; others allow their materials to 'grow' themselves according to chance, like living things, as in the case of Ela Bauer; still others simply collect natural material and work it into their own unique craft. All, however, share a quality that seems to have been formed by organic process rather than human hand.

The second chapter here, in a very different way, also presents makers who contest and at times invert the conventions of traditional jewellery. These "Playthings and Parodies" share a sense of fun, deflating the pomp and ceremony of some more traditional work, and challenging expectations. They play with scale, as in the case of Marc Monzo; they juxtapose incongruous elements, they draw upon surreal imagery and the colour and movement of toys; they question the assumptions behind the wearing of diamonds and gold. Tiny creatures like Noa Nadir's and Felieke van der Leest's climb upon the body; small kinetic elements invite the wearer to play. They are not necessarily frivolous; as the work of long-established maker Sigurd Bronger shows here as a case in point, a light touch can be used to engage the wearer both intellectually and through laughter. What many of these pieces have in common, then, is a sense of inclusivity, an invitation to interact and enjoy, rather than revere.

Although some of the works shown in the following section share this playful edge (it would be difficult to view Silke Fleischer's perfectly executed, silver bag of chips with an entirely straight face), they differ in the relationship between wearer and piece. More stand-alone objects than conventional jewellery, these "Artworks and Objects" probe the boundaries of ornamentation, functioning as much as tiny sculptures as they do as wearable items. Many of them are figurative, in contrast to the more abstracted, simple shapes of conventional jewellery; they incorporate or reproduce objects from the everyday world, or represent the human form. At times, the possibility of wearing the pieces is questionable; many are as much designed to be shown in a gallery space as worn upon the body.

In contrast to this, the pieces shown in "Layers of Adornment" each have a unique and challenging relationship with the wearer; the questions they raise are precisely concerned with the ways in which the body, clothing, and jewellery interact and intersect. At what point does a decorative accessory cross into the territory of apparel? And where is the line between an object worn on the body, and the impression that object leaves behind? Pieces morph to the form of the wearer; alter or append themselves to items of clothing; and even leave visible marks on the skin. Makers such as Tiffany Parbs and Madeleine Furness take this notion to the extreme, so that pinpricks, burns, and scars become a part of the work itself. Others shown here, such as Husam El Odeh and Rheanna Lingham, are at perhaps a less extreme end of the spectrum, but their works tread an interesting line between clothing and jewellery, moving forward not only in their own medium but also in the realm of fashion design.

Following on from the concerns raised by the preceding chapter, "Small Things in a Wide World" examines jewelleries that look beyond the notion of adornment to a broader context. Jewellery is perhaps typically thought of either as something timeless, to be handed through generations untouched by the changing world; or otherwise, as something disposable, a costume piece to last a season. In either case, the wearer is rarely concerned with the relationship that piece might have to the world in which it was created. Yet jewellery is knit up in a variety of broader concerns, from the sourcing of materials to its influence on concepts of beauty. The makers here engage with social, political, or geographical contexts; some use jewellery as a means of record, representing the social environment they find themselves in, incorporating at times the imagery and material that constitutes a consumer, media-driven society. Others bear testimony to specific political histories and conditions. The work of Shari Pierce is singled out as a testament to the possibility of making a small, fragile statement count in the face of difficult realities.

The final chapter in this volume narrows the focus again to concentrate upon the ways in which contemporary makers draw upon jewellery's own long and fascinating history. These "Cameos and Keepsakes" address the uses to which jewellery has been put in the past – as *memento mori*, as cameo portraits, as a way to keep a loved one close, in lockets and treasured gifts. Some do so in their form, finding new ways to make personalised cameo pieces, like Cassandra Chilton, or setting old jewels in new ways like Karl Fritsch and Eija Mustonen; others take the concepts of the past and rework them in contemporary settings, like the beautiful, understated pieces of Melanie Bilenker, tiny portraits of domesticity which recall the Victorian use of human hair as a remembrance. Yet others make reference in their technique to the conventions of the past, reviving and celebrating traditional crafts such as goldsmithing and gem setting. In all of these pieces, there is an interaction between a varied, inspiring tradition, and a contemporary approach.

This last section, then, attenuates something that is true to some extent of all of the jewellers in this book – jewellers who are working within, around, and beyond an age-old craft. There are works here that can be firmly placed within the bounds of that craft, refining, honing and updating traditional forms and methods, while others cross over into a range of disciplines, from fine art to sculpture to mechanics. Here are small, deeply personal statements, and elsewhere, social and political concerns; some of these pieces are challenging, provocative, even difficult, while others are playful and comic. And none of these poles are mutually exclusive; what is laid out in the pages that follow showcases the broad, ever-expanding field of contemporary practice.

Lin Cheung

WEAR, WEARING, WORN: THE TRANSITIONS OF JEWELS TO JEWELLERY

We are familiar with contemporary jewellery as a vehicle for makers to express their artistic thought, material concerns, attitudes to society, beliefs, fashion trends, cultural viewpoints, customs, and rituals – to list just a few examples. These avenues of 'designed expression' are common to art, fashion, conceptual and traditional jewellery; serving to locate, within each category, an appropriate expressive symbol for use in the construction of one's sense of self-image. Despite jewellery containing these different forms of 'designed expression' – that ultimately communicate the values of the maker or designer – all jewellery also has the endless capacity to hold personal, unique meaning for the wearer, eventually defining the piece beyond its initial design and conception. By wearing, owning and interacting with jewellery, we breathe new life into it. We activate it and set it on a life-long journey to collect and absorb its surroundings. The jewellery that sits finished in a maker's studio, displayed in a gallery or for sale in a shop window, is entirely different to the jewellery that we wear, use and cherish amongst our personal possessions. 'New' jewellery has yet to find its vocation; yet to acquire the associations and values of a person's life to shape its identity. Perhaps this jewellery could be termed 'jewellery-to-be', where the role of the object is predefined and inevitable, but has yet to be meaningfully connected to someone to complete its official status as full jewellery. A new noun is required to adequately define jewellery in a state of limbo.

The ways in which a piece of jewellery acquires meaning is played out and reflected upon by makers that have considered the life of their creations beyond their realm as artist-makers. Contemplating what is to become of the life of a fledgling jewel poses many questions. How does the piece get 'discovered'? How does someone 'begin' to wear a piece, interpret it and find a way of attaching his or her own meanings to it? Who buys it? Who wears it? And for what reason? How closely do the intentions of the maker meet with the values of the wearer, known or unknown to the maker?

The work of Manuel Vilhena conveys a vivid sense of self-discovery. The components of each piece are compiled with apparent ease and there is no discernable order or system to speak of. It is not too farfetched to think that these pieces may have 'built' themselves, tangled together

1. Manuel Vilhena
Brooch
Amber, 18ct gold, cotton
2005
Courtesy Galerie Marzee

2. Manuel Vilhena
Brooch
Bone, iron, silver,
steel, cotton
2004
Courtesy Galerie Marzee

entirely by accident and found, by a busy roadside or washed up on a shore line, as a collection of broken fragments. The maker's ego is not apparent, and neither is any obvious message or subversive code – all common constituents of contemporary jewellery. This is, of course, their appeal. Vilhena's work is purely of the visual and tactile – it is what it is: an entirely 'honest' jewel. Discovered by the wearer in this timeless way, each item is open to interpretation and the wearer is left simply to wear the piece and to attribute his or her own meanings onto it. Similarly, the work of Iris Bodemer also holds a strong sense of intuitiveness. With every fine line, unusual shape and nuance in colour used, it engages the composition of a self-image, as described by one wearer: "... the little pebble is 'me', wandering and holding on to the earth. My everyday setting is one of grey suits, and this piece of jewellery makes an impact."[1] With limitless varieties of materials to hand, it demands integrity and a keen eye on the part of the maker to spot potential combinations; just as it would call for great restraint and discipline if, for a souvenir, one were asked to take home just a single, special pebble from a beach full of endless possibilities. The process of selecting, then, takes on meaning.

The term 'jewellery-to-be' also carries with it notions of the jewel itself being physically incomplete; requiring something tangible, as well as emotional or intellectual, from the wearer to develop this part of its final meaning. Like an empty chair waiting to be 'completed' by its

3. Iris Bodemer
(left)
Pendant 99
Silver, aragonite
(middle)
Silver, citrine
(right)
Silver, peridot
2002

4. Iris Bodemer
Neckpiece
Silver, aquamarine, pebble
Worn by Marijke Snijders
2001
Photography: Michiel Heffels
Courtesy Galerie Marzee

owner; jewellery is also wanting of a wearer. Without a finger, a ring is an object with a hole; a necklace adopts a meaningless shape without the armature of a neck and earrings do not make sense until the illusion is complete by hiding its findings behind an earlobe. Gijs Bakker's *Everybody's friend* ring, 1994, requires the wearer to decide which loop determines the wearability – and thus the definition – of the piece, by selecting the correct size of ring to fit their finger. In the same way, Rolf Sachs' *Strip Bracelet*, 1995, is essentially reliant on physical intervention to complete its meaning as jewellery. The 'bracelet' is presented as a smooth, flat sheet of silver, daring the wearer to first disturb the pristine surface; in doing so, the hands of the wearer complete the phase of jewel to jewellery. Dinie Besems' *Tear Ring*, 1995, poetically describes the emotional investment in a jewel before it can begin to acquire meaning. A single teardrop is shed onto the ring to complete it with a temporary gemstone. Too many tears or not enough would not result in the same formation of a perfect gemstone. The accurate distilling of sentimental value can be paramount to the meaning of jewellery.

The commission process provides a direct route for significant and personal meanings to be worked into a jewel. The intimate, sentimental value of a jewel to a wearer is distinctively realised in the corporeal work of Gerd Rothmann. *Family Necklace* (for the Schöbinger family), 1998, consists of a necklace of small, gold discs, randomly marked with fingerprints. Meaning is constructed and consolidated for the wearer through the fingerprints of her family, "So when I wear the necklace, my family is with me. The necklace caresses my neck and with it, my whole family, whom I love dearly."[2] Proof of love, commitment and family values physically define the necklace; the unique is evidenced. In another, more practical commission, Gijs Bakker appeals directly to the diplomatic role and formidable personality of the former secretary of state for the US, Madeleine K Albright. *Liberty Brooch*, 1997, depicts a linear outline of the head of the Statue of Liberty; in place of the eyes are set two watches: "One upside down for Mrs Albright to know how long her appointment will last and her visitor at what time to leave."[3] But what of the other jewellery we see Ms Albright wearing? These items are clearly not by the hand of the

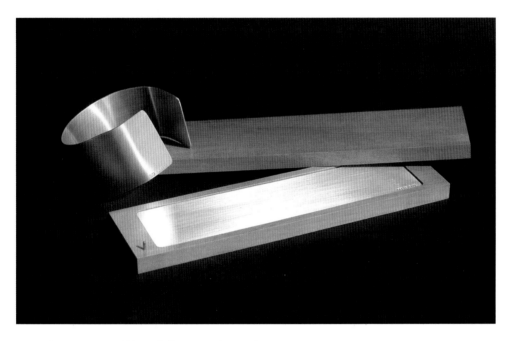

5. Rolf Sachs
Strip Bracelet
Silver
1995

6. Gijs Bakker
Everybody's friend
Ring
Silver 925
1994
Photography: Ton Werhoven

7. Dinie Besems
Tear Ring
Silver
1995
Photography: Thijs Wolzak

same artist and yet they occupy the same space as the brooch. In their discreetness, we cannot see with the same eyes what may be hidden behind this private language. What meaning do these items hold for Ms Albright? To inquire after them would seem too personal, too direct and perhaps rude; an intrusion into a revelation that is meant for the wearer only, and upon asking, one suspects that the question would be quickly dismissed. A new tactic is required to penetrate this jewellery of a different language.

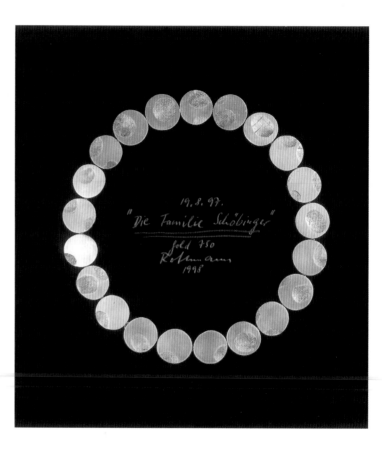

8. Gijs Bakker
Liberty Brooch
Silver 925, watches
1997
Executed by: Pauline Barendse
Photography: Rien Bazen
Courtesy Helen Drutt,
Philadelphia

9. Gerd Rothman
Family Necklace (for the
Schöbinger family)
Gold
1998
Photography: Wilfried Petzi

The majority of the jewellery we see worn and in use is not too dissimilar to the items belonging to Ms Albright. They are generally the mass-made, small, gold glints and silver punctuation marks of a person's life. Blended into their daily attire, they go unnoticed at times, even to the wearer. In Mah Rana's ongoing project *Meanings and Attachments*, begun 2002, the question one would like to put to Ms Albright about her 'personal' jewellery is the same and only question put to the participants of Rana's project. *Meanings and Attachments* forms a series of photographs and documented interviews of people about the stories and histories attached to their jewellery. Photographed and represented in this way, it commands our attention and forces us to look again, and in turn reconsider our assumptions about the wearer and of course their jewellery. They welcome us to wonder about the life of each wearer and in doing so, we begin to construct for ourselves some of the fundamental meanings behind the wearing of

jewellery. The overall message is one of unity in our uniqueness. These are people that have chosen for themselves, or received as gifts, jewels that contain stories, personal histories, associations with loved ones and significant events that have transformed their 'traditional' jewels into jewellery.

Kim Buck deliberately pays tribute to these conventional forms of jewellery. Whilst Buck's contemporary goldsmithing designs are a world away from traditional types of jewellery, in a recent series of work, he readily acknowledges that the reasons why people commission, buy, wear and own jewellery, remains identical and "untouchable" for both forms of jewellery. The sharp outlines of an anchor chain, a pair of pearl earrings, a crucifix, a heart, all appear in the surface of gold and silver brooches like a form of hieroglyphic 'jewellery sign language'. These traditional

 12. Kim Buck
(from left to right)
4 Brooches *Gold Cross in Anchorchain*
Solitaire Ring
Gold Heart in Anchorchain
Earrings with Pearls
Gold 750
4 x 4 x 0.4 cm each
2003
Photography: Ole Akhøj

13. Kim Buck
String of Pearls with Golden Lock
Brooches, silver and gold 750
4 x 4 x 0.4 cm each
2003
Photography: Ole Akhøj

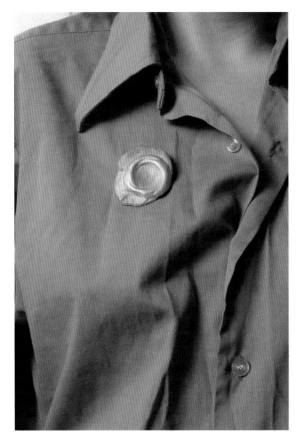

14. Karl Fritsch
Brooch
Gold 750, brass
1995
Photography: Karl Fritsch

15. Karl Fritsch
Ring
Gold 900, gold 333
1993
Photography: Karl Fritsch

signs and symbols, recognised universally, come fully furnished with their own clichés. The title of Buck's series *it is the thought that counts*, 2001, is translated literally into jewellery-like objects that deny the receiver of such gifts the ability to wear the precious items in a conventional way. As the phrase suggests, the real value is in the wearing of them in the heart and mind.

Not all jewellery acquires enough meaning or shine to last in its relationship with its owner. To the contrary, meaning can also result in unwanted jewellery. For whatever reason – perhaps through changing trends in fashion, a death, divorce, over-accumulation, or an immediate financial need which temporarily outweighs the sentimental value of a ring, brooch or necklace – jewellery becomes parted from its owner and can find its way to, amongst other lonely places, a pawnbroker. For one series of work, Karl Fritsch bought gold jewellery from pawnshops, with the intention of using them as raw material for casting. Instead, touched and influenced by the melancholic air of some of these broken and neglected pieces, Fritsch nurtured and re-worked them into a new kind of jewellery. As Fritsch puts it, by acting as "jewellery psychiatrist", these pieces are spared their final demise and reincarnation into new gold. A broken ring shank is mended with a large casting of a kneaded piece of wax. Pressed and shaped into place, it does the job of fixing the ring as intuitively and practically as one would stop a wobble to a table by inserting a folded paper napkin under the shortest leg. With other pieces, as if not wishing the 'naked' areas of a jewel to be exposed, missing stones or pearls are replaced with small lumps of gold. Fritsch respectfully attends to the jewellery with an act of necessity. This sense of necessity is at its strongest when we see the renewed item then pinned onto the chest or slipped over the finger of a wearer. The jewels by themselves look accidental, uncontrolled or even a mistake; on a person they look deliberate: refreshed, repaired and back in use.

When jewellery is off the body temporarily, it is often carefully and deliberately placed amongst our other personal possessions. The lateral work of Laura Potter explores the means by which people store special items of jewellery. A process of reverse psychology is used that focuses attention away from the jewel itself to observe the valuing of it. *Ring Frame*, 2005, appears to be a small picture frame. It is not until we discover that the method by which it hangs relies on a piece of jewellery to complete the necessary 'hook' to hold the frame to the wall, that we realise it is in fact a secret hiding place for a treasured ring. The location and memory of the jewellery is kept safe and intact via the image installed in the front of the frame. The symbiotic relationship of jewellery and wearer is reinforced. Potter having also noticed that people store their jewellery for safekeeping in the bottom of a drawer, *Safesock*, 2005, is designed for storing earrings. Each pair of miniature socks is considerately linked together to prevent loss or displacement of a matching pair. At the same time, the familiar knitted construction neatly camouflages them within a drawer full of other socks, away from prying eyes. Maria Militsi also invites us indirectly to meditate on the preciousness of jewellery. Prompted by the alluring

16. Laura Potter
Safesock
Wool
2005
Photography:
Michiel Heffels

17. Laura Potter
Ring Frame
Birch plywood
2005
Photography:
Laura Potter

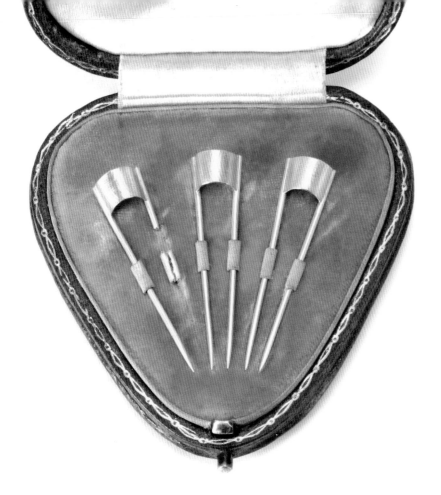

emotional space found inside vintage jewellery boxes, Militsi dexterously crafts new jewels to fit the space the original item once inhabited. Each new piece, like a small hermit-like creature making a new home, responds accordingly to its surroundings, picking up the ghostly traces left behind to define parts of its form and character. Militsi's work encourages us to nurture and to take care of jewellery to express that the value of an item of jewellery can also be found in its relationship to where it is kept.

Contemporary jewellery is not often seen worn by 'ordinary' people going about their daily business. In an effort to remedy this and to widen the public's knowledge of contemporary jewellery, a project run by Galerie Marzee in The Netherlands invites women from surrounding local towns and cities to choose and wear for a day a piece of jewellery from the gallery. The concept of this project is perhaps as close as we can get to a perfect world for contemporary jewellery. By photographically documenting the pieces being worn and reading the reasons why these women have chosen to wear their particular pieces, the jewels are a step closer to becoming jewellery. The meanings of the jewels are, if only momentarily, completed. Common to all the reasons why the women chose the pieces they did are thoughts about suitability, flattery, appropriateness and inappropriateness; who they are, what they do, who they want to be, their interests and what they say and want to say about themselves – or, as the cultural theorist Ted Polhemus succinctly encapsulates it: "jewellery as adjective".⁴ *Chalk Chain*, 2004, by Dinie Besems, began its life as a conceptual exhibition piece and was expected to remain

20. (from left to right)
Ane Koczorowski
Visual Design Teacher and
Visual Artist
Jewellery: Manuel Vilhena
Brooch
Jap I, 2004
Ebony, steel
14 x 7.2 x 2 cm
Ring, 2004
Ebony, amber
5.4 x 4.4 x 2.2 cm

Ada Valk
Schiedam Municipality
Councillor
Jewellery: Miriam Verbeek
Necklace, 2002
wool, 27 cm ø

Deborah Lens
Cultural Education Policy
Advisor, Commercial Artistic
Leader of Youth Theatre,
School, Agency De Teerstoof.
Necklace: Vera Siemund
2003
Enamelled copper, silver, glass
33.5 x 24 x 5 cm
Ring: Karin Seufert
2004, Silver, colorit
1.5 x 2.1 x 2.6 cm
Photography:
Pieter Huybrechts
Courtesy Galerie Marzee

this way, as is often the case with conceptual work. But for one of the owners of this necklace, the wearing of it is not only essential in continuing its conceptual life (transient marks and traces of chalk dust are left on the wearer's clothing); wear also creates a value and a personal meaning for the piece. By photographing herself in different places wearing the necklace, a record of its existence is built. A memory of the event, the place and the emotions are recorded, all adding to the new life of the necklace.

If we can describe jewellery to be a language – a tool for communication designed to express, without words, our abstract inner selves – then to understand the wearing and meaning of jewellery to its fullest, it is perhaps appropriate to look beyond the jewel and to study its associations and environments academically and anthropologically. By sociologically observing jewellery's constituents, seeking out its motivations and collecting key patterns of 'jewellery behaviour' we can perhaps uncover empirical data to be researched further. Achieving this requires impartiality, and venturing into that long-forgotten world of traditional jewellery, frequently characterised by many as 'banal and non-descript'. We need not fear this 'dystopian' world of jewellery. If this jewellery was once the impetus for more interesting, better designed contemporary jewellery, then to study its prevailing usage can contribute to a better understanding of the wearing of all jewellery. It is in this very world of 'traditional' jewellery, a forgotten majority, that 'jewellery-to-be' is being most readily transformed into meaningful jewellery. The significance of revisiting these items of jewellery lies in engaging with wearers of all jewellery that has taken on extra meaning and value, beyond what was originally designed onto and into the object at the time of its completion. By observing how and what additional values are placed onto jewellery through the wearing and owning of it, we can aim to fully address the part that contemporary jewellery can play towards a greater understanding of the personal and social values made manifest through all objects. I propose a new jewellery utopia where it is of little consequence whether a jewel is a one-off artwork or a mass-produced item; both require the unique intervention of diverse human experiences by the wearer or owner to complete its transition from jewel to jewellery.

1. Snijders, Marijke, quoted in *Marzee Magazine*, no. 19, The Netherlands: Galerie Marzee, 2001, p. 11.
2. Schöbinger, Barbara, quoted in *Gerd Rothmann – Schmuck*, Ostfildern-Ruit: Hatje Cantz, 2002, p. 114.
3. Bakker, Gijs, in a letter to Helen W Drutt English 12 November 1997, quoted in Wendy Steiner, "Brooching Power", *Brooching it diplomatically – A tribute to Madeleine K Albright*, Philadelphia: Helen Drutt, 1998, p. 14.
4. Polhemus, Ted, "The adorned ape", *Koru2 International Contemporary Jewellery*, Lappeenranta, Finland: South Karelia Art Museum, 2006, p. 13.

21. Dinie Besems
Chalk Chain
Worn by Claartje Keur
Chalk
2004
Photography: Claartje Keur

NATURAL SELECTION

kirsten Bak

ela bauer

julie blyfield

sebastian buescher

karl fritsch

constanze schreiber

kirsten bak

Creating unique wearable artefacts that inspire the imagination, Bak's work is informed by the notion of reconstruction – of recycling, reusing, rethinking and representing. Utilising a combination of natural and artificial materials including plastic, steel and silver, Bak's *Rekonstruktion* series of brooches feature details from porcelain figures. The figures are cast and remade in thin plastic, with the pieces later dissected and united in an abstracted fashion. Bak exhibits an interest in volume and form, with less concern for details and ornament: "I believe we focus a lot on the shell and seldom look beneath", says Bak. "The details capture us and prevent us from looking further, we forget to play with our imagination."

Bak's intriguing *Unicated* ring series made from wood and plastic follows the same theme, with the rings literally taking their form from tree boughs. Bak gathers forks of plane trees, selecting sections where the branch divides into two or more. The sections are hollowed out, leaving behind a thin and fragile residual surface used to create the rings. Bak allows nature to shape her forms, with the wood patterning and markings forming the ornamental facet of the jewellery, while a layer of stabilising plastic sheaths the exterior. Bak explains humbly of her organic pieces: "Each ring tells you the story of a tree."

1. *Unicated*
Plastic, wood rings
2006

2. *Unicated*
Wood ring
2006

3. *Unicated*
Plastic, wood rings
2006

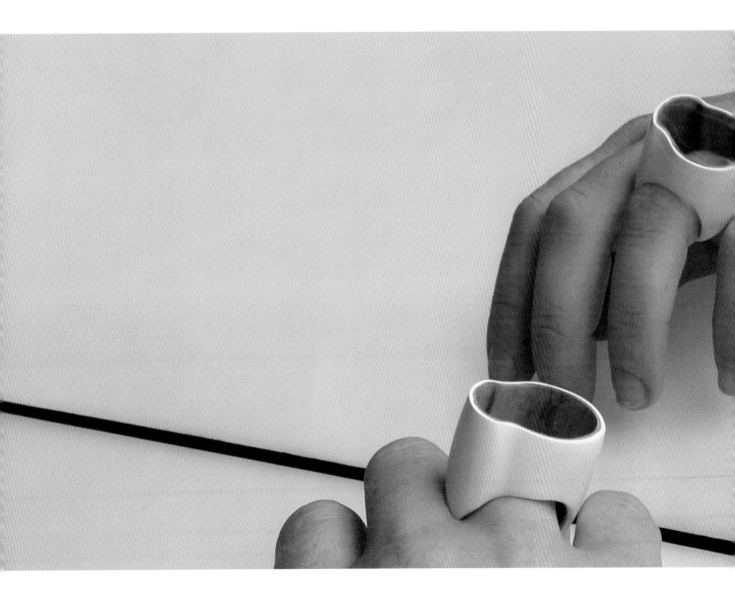

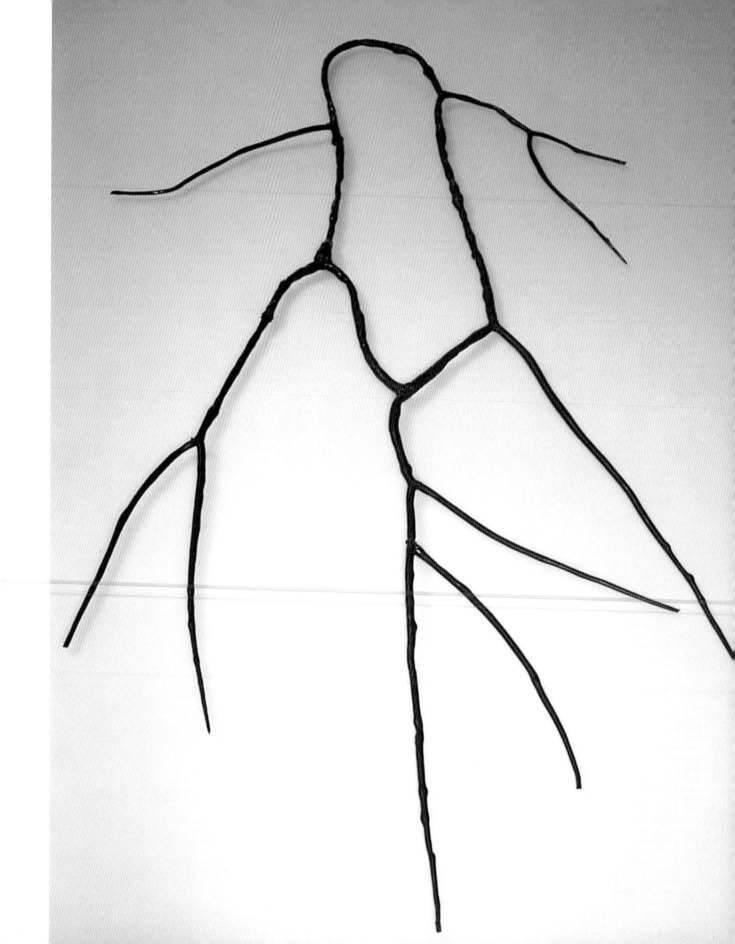

1. Necklace
Silicone, pigment, thread
2004

2. Ring
Silicone, coral, silver
2005

ela bauer

3. Necklace
Silicone, pigment,
copper mesh
2003

Starting from the notion that nothing is clearly defined – that events, actions, objects and emotions are open to interpretation and unstable in character – the work of Ela Bauer is informed by concepts of flux and development, situating itself as a representation of the ambiguous. Inspired by the uncertain, 'liquid' aspects of reality, Bauer works with the indeterminate to create jewelleries overtly reflective of growth principles and evolving concepts of sequence and process. Preoccupied by perceptions of continuous change and movement, and by the multiplication of cells and organisms within the natural environment, she has formed a collection that mirrors both aesthetically and conceptually the laws of nature. Via the manipulation and re-formation of amorphous silicone rubber, jewelleries are cast, stitched, and drenched in vibrant, piercing hues. Hybrid in their aesthetics, they remain indistinct, persistently contesting classification or definition. Appearing elastic, semi-transparent and soft to the touch, each piece, whether a bulbous ring or sprouting necklace, is defined by its colouring which, determining to a great extent the meaning and atmosphere of the work, plays a central role in its conception and reception. Details are formed from layers of acidic greens and bloody reds, painted onto the stained silicone, highlighting the formation and shape of the rubber itself. Other works form from a collection of silicone cells, mutating awkwardly into objects that defy conventional perceptions of jewellery design and wearability. Connected by delicate threads, these cells are sewn by hand, symbolising the eternal human attempt to create, mend, protect and reconstruct. Bringing together the modern (silicone) and traditional (the act of sewing), Bauer seeks to strengthen the impact, drawing upon the silicone surface with the needle and thread to create "veins, rivers, paths and scares".

1. *Embroidery* collection
Brooch
Silver
2006
Photography: Grant Hancock

2. *Pressed desert plant* series
Brooches
Silver, enamel, wax
2005
Photography: Grant Hancock

JULIE blyfield

Like delicate specimens from the natural world, the jewellery of Australian designer Julie Blyfield references explicitly both personal and social histories. Inspired by collections of botany, old floral embroideries and pressed plants, they are faithful in shape, texture, form and colour to the precepts of nature, the materials worked to appear soft and wholly organic. Blyfield utilises various metal raising techniques to work oxidised sterling silver into three-dimensional forms, which are then pierced, folded and threaded together, and combined with enamel paint and wax. Working annealed metal sheets with fine steel tools, she creates surface texture and pattern, celebrating entirely any natural distortions or imperfections that may arise throughout the process. "I enjoy the transformation of the flat sheet into three-dimensional forms", explains Blyfield. "I texture and hammer the silver sheet with small steel tools while at the same time, supporting the pierced silver in 'pitch'. As the metal is chased, it hardens and moves and curls up in all manner of unpredictable ways – this is a process that suits perfectly the forms that I seek to create." By applying colour directly to these 'pressed plant' pieces, Blyfield seeks to reflect the warmth and faded, muted tones of actual plant specimens; in this way, botanical imagery, which has been represented in the design and process of jewellery making throughout history, is presented in a contemporary context.

1. Ring
Porcelain, crystal, sik, thread,
amazonite, pearl
0.2 x 0.2 cm
2006

2. *Pretty Poison* ring
Silver, ebony, amber, jade,
resin, deadly nightshade
4 x 2.5 cm
2005

sebastian Buescher

Unsatisfied by the typical functions of traditional jewellery, Sebastian Buescher's designs are conceived as expressive, communicative tools, intended to serve as an outlet for specifically personal ideas and contemplation. As a form of escape from a rule-driven reality and the banalities and regularities of everyday life, his pieces exist as small sculptural objects infused with memory and meaning, extending jewellery design into the surreal realm of the non-functional, conceptual art object. The maker explains: "My art jewellery is not made to be worn, and the wearing of it by no means justifies its existence. This is my idea of total freedom of expression, simply because the function of a functional object has been removed. For me, there is nothing more pleasurable than playing with the absurd and nonsensical notions that I confront myself with." In Buescher's world, everything wants to be what it is not, and nothing has to function as it should; his jewelleries refute categorisation or justification. Playing out notions of the absurd and nonsensical, in this designer's curious world objects morph and mutate, adopting peculiar characteristics, taking on strange, unknown forms. "I do what I can to take things out of their traditional context and to place them in a new landscape", explains Buescher. "I do this because I can and because I need to find some sort of escape from this calculated, controlled, monotone world where sense and logic rule. In my world, nothing has to make sense."

Attending to the passage of time and the evolution of the natural environment, Buescher draws inspiration from an eclectic and eccentric range of sources – from archaeology, history and nature, as well as his own imagination, referencing the processes and forms of nature, which repeat themselves in the shape of nests, pods, eggs and anthills. Here, reconstituted bone, sea urchin spines, insects, human ashes, teeth and animal skulls are juxtaposed with precious metals (gold and silver), ceramics, corals, resins and paper, as well as both natural and synthetic fabrics. Materials that fascinate are combined with those chosen for their inherent meaning and allegory. Second-hand toys, inherited jewellery and photographs resonate with notions of time, memory, duality and personal faith, forming a collection heavy in both personal association and symbolism.

3

3. Brooch
Silver spoon, silver, porcelain
3.5 x 9 cm
2006

 4. *Pregnant Tree Boy*
Brooch
Wood, silver, porcelain, pearl,
glass, black widow spider
2006

5. *Spork*
Hand object
Spoon, fork, paint,
wisdom tooth
10 cm
2005

6
7

6. *Fragile*
Hand object
Coral, resin, thread,
urchin spines
7 x 5 cm
2005

7. *365 rings*
Silver, gold
3 x 2 cm
2005

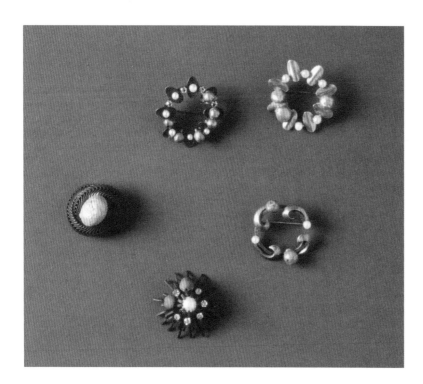

1. 5 Brooches
Gold, silver, brass, pearls,
glass
1996

Karl Fritsch

While studying at Munich Academy, Karl Fritsch was drawn to making "disgusting looking jewellery". He explains: "I wanted it to draw more attention than a pretty piece of jewellery would – this is after all one of jewellery's issues – attention and attraction." And his designs, predominantly rings, certainly catch the eye. Expertly crafted, yet not working within the usual framework of shape and colour existing in jewellery, Fritsch's rings feature unexpected combinations of organic and archetypal forms, smooth and rough edges and clumps of coloured glass stones. Playing with the traditional notion of jewellery as 'beautiful', Fritsch creates unconventional pieces that win attention through alternative means. "I don't want my jewellery to look designed", Fritsch notes. "They have organic, undefined shapes, made out of silver and painted dark grey. The idea is that amongst all the pretty jewellery something ugly can attract even more attention and support the wearer."

Fritsch's latest works, featuring bulky and uninhibited shapes alongside vivid glass stones, are initially formed from wax by hand. A key aspect of Fritsch's designs is that as the rings are worn, the silver and gold components will change, becoming shinier and more polished, so that the wearer is essentially transforming the ring through constant use. "I like my jewellery to have an individual life with the people who wear it", explains Fritsch. "The universality of ornaments impresses me and stimulates me to make jewellery I would like to see people wearing."

2. Pendant
Gold 900, gold 333
1995
Photography: Karl Fritsch

3 **4**

3. Ring
Gold, emeralds
2.5 x 4 x 2.5 cm
2005

4. Ring
White gold, silver, rubies,
sapphires, emeralds,
carnelian, amethyst,
peridot, garnet
2.5 x 4.5 x 1.5 cm
2005

1. *Marie*
Brooch
Fur, lead, silver, steel
14 x 8 x 2 cm
2005
Photography: Edo Knipers

constanze schreiber

Embracing the irregular, Constanze Schreiber works with a range of expressive materials, from the conventional (copper, corals, leather and acrylic), to the obscure (horsehair, crushed glass and soap). Experimenting with both material and form, her work can be placed at the interface of art and design, aesthetically unusual yet irrefutably wearable. Infused with the tribal, primal, mythological and metaphoric, it is often surreal and highly symbolic. Exploring the history of ritual and superstition, pieces effectively blend the everyday with core universal symbols such as the skull (death/morality), anchor (hope) and mirror (vanity/truth/imagination), forming works unique in their design. Made from a combination of crushed blue glass, silver and plastic, a three-dimensional hand serves as an unusual pendant; a mirror is formed from felt and silver, the reflective glass replaced by a worn mother of peal skull-shaped slab; a brooch is born from netting and coloured corals, shaped as a weathered anchor, dangling from a silver disk designed to be pinned to the wearer's breast. Seeking to examine the ways in which we attempt to deal with and accept fear and anxiety, Schreiber taps into the protective aspects of traditional jewelleries such as the amulet or talisman (symbolising good health and good luck), contemplating notions of life and death in a collection of evocative jewelleries. Returning continually to themes of myth and mortality she employs a vocabulary of forms conceived to speak of higher values, to question, challenge and provoke. In her work, the usual becomes unusual, her pieces embodying obscured representations of reality.

2. *Eugenie*
Brooch
Fur, lead, silver, steel
12 x 8.5 x 0.2 cm
Photography: Edo Knipers

3. *The Mirrow*
Object
Shell, felt, silver
30 x 16 x 12 cm
2004
Photography: Shinji Otani

4. *Elisabeth*
Necklace
Fur, lead, silver
27.5 x 21 x 2 cm
2005
Photography: Edo Knipers

PLAYTHINGS AND PARODIES

Maisie Broadhead

Sigurd Bronger

Arthur Hash

Craig Isaac

Felieke van der Leest

Lindsey Mann

Marc Monzó

Noa Nadir

Ted Noten

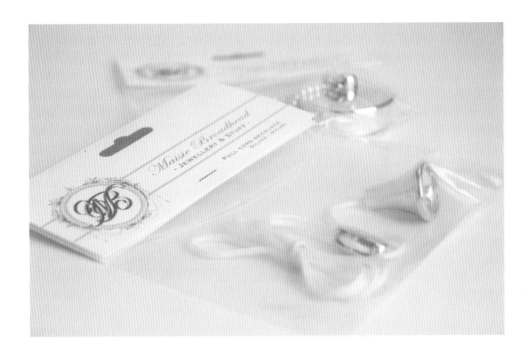

mAisie broadHead

Maisie Broadhead's *Bathroom* series is an elegantly simple, yet immediately accessible collection of jewellery. Taking the most recognisable and iconic fixtures and fittings from the everyday English bathroom – "objects that we use and touch daily, and often discard their real worth" – she turns them into jewellery that is both precious and desirable.

Using electroforming or silver casting processes, dependent on the object, bathplugs, overflow fittings and pull cords are all given new life and new worth, disguised as refined silver jewellery. "With these pieces it's very important to me that the design of the objects remain instantly recognisable, down to the smallest detail of how a bath plug hangs from its chain, or how the cord of a pull-switch is knotted. By changing the material, but more importantly its context, this familiar object becomes totally transformed. It almost feels like I'm giving these poor old personalities a moment of glory, celebration and importance."

The *Bathroom* collection also continues Broadhead's pre-occupation with how the presentation of work must be integral to the work itself. The pieces are presented in their own, labelled, individual polythene bags, akin to those we see hanging from the shelves of the local hardware shop. Maisie affectionately classes her genre as "Jewellery & Stuff", moving freely between worn pieces like *Bathroom*, to gallery exhibitions such as *Gestures*, where she created cast-silver translations of Bruno Munari's dictionary of Italian hand-gestures and displayed them as specimens alongside photography and text. "Whether I'm creating jewellery, or objects for a gallery, I find I'm often trying to achieve a balance between elegance and humour."

1. *Plug & Overflow*
Brooch
Silver, rubber plug
2006
Photography: Jazzy Jack

2. *Pull Cord*
Necklace
Silver, nylon cord
Detail of Bags
2006
Photography: Jazzy Jack

1. Brooch
24ct & 18ct gold, acrylic,
glass, silver
7 cm
2004

siGurd BroNGeR

Setting a ring with a tiny diamond and a magnifying glass, Bronger is perhaps incorporating the peering gesture of an ungrateful recipient of a proposal – "is that it?" – or deflating the 'bigger is better' mentality of bling. Yet the piece itself has the preciousness and intricacy of an antique instrument for navigation or mapping, simultaneously parodying the notion of jewel as treasured status symbol, and creating a new kind of object to be treasured.

Bringing his technical expertise to bear upon smiley faces, miniature space hoppers, and other everyday objects, Sigurd Bronger creates objects that are at once aesthetically pleasing and entertaining. By taking ordinary objects like sponges and soap, used and overlooked daily, and fashioning jewellery from them, Bronger confounds typical expectations of jewellery as something durable and precious, applying a sophisticated craftsmanship to that which is disposable and commonplace. Both historically and in cultures throughout the world, jewellery has been made from what is found, from anything and everything; and while it frequently serves a symbolic function, beyond the purpose of simple decorative adornment, it seems that the particular way that jewellery in contemporary society signifies is, more often than not, a transparent demonstration of wealth. That is to say, that while in certain cultures the wearing of a particular piece, or a particular quantity of jewellery for example might signify wealth, the gold chains and dripping diamonds of the conspicuous consumer are both symbol and embodiment of that which is symbolised. It is this, perhaps, that Bronger sends up, confronting our expectations of what a piece of jewellery should 'mean'. Someone coming close to one of these works to assess just how valuable the piece is, and how valid the wearer in consequence, is likely to be squirted with water in the face.

Each piece is presented in its own beechwood box, "encased", as Bronger puts it, so that "the constituent elements take part in an internal dialogue". These, then, are both discrete singular objects, designed to be upheld and admired, as well as wearable jewellery, their fixings executed as ingeniously as the pieces themselves. Combining materials into meticulously crafted, tactile artefacts, he creates pieces whose absurdity lends them a warmth and humour.

If Bronger's gaze is wry and satirical, it is also child-like in its fascination with machines, with the intricacies of now-redundant mechanisms which can be taken apart, piece by piece, each part lovingly crafted, polished, and re-assembled. He delights in the exposure of mechanical parts, with the curiosity of a child dissecting a toy. The juxtaposition of aesthetics and function – a piece of jewellery which is also a handy *Watering Instrument*, yet recalls a clown's water-squirting joke-shop flower – is a source of humour, suggestive of use but ultimately redundant. That very juxtaposition, and redundancy, betrays Bronger's nostalgia for a time when the functional object was also, in his eyes, a beautiful one. In a sense, then, he is reversing the notion of 'form follows function', whereby the beauty of an object arises from its pure functionality. Here, functional objects are inserted or incorporated into that which is purely decorative – jewellery.

Inversions, disjunctions, juxtapositions; interactive elements, a sense of play; jewellery can call upon these elements to bring pleasure to the wearer, to create a private joke that can be shared with others, and carried around all day. The very presence of the unexpected, of a joke so lovingly crafted and delicately presented, invites wearer and viewer alike to laugh.

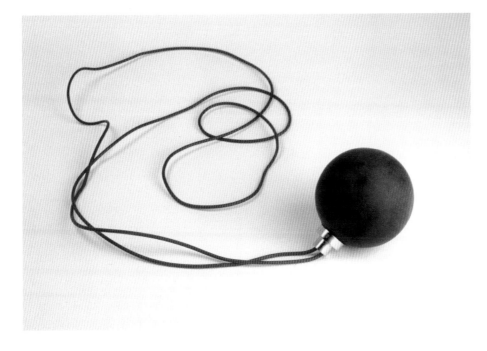

 2. Watering Instrument
Brooch
Natural sponge, brass,
steel, rubber
2001

3. *Ball Necklace*
18ct gold, rubber cord,
bakelite ball
4 cm
2005

4. *Magnifying Ring*
18ct gold, lenses, diamond,
chromed brass
3 x 1.5 cm
2005

5. *Smiley Brooch*
Balloon, chromed brass,
rubber
15 cm
2004

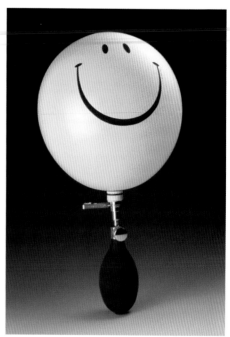

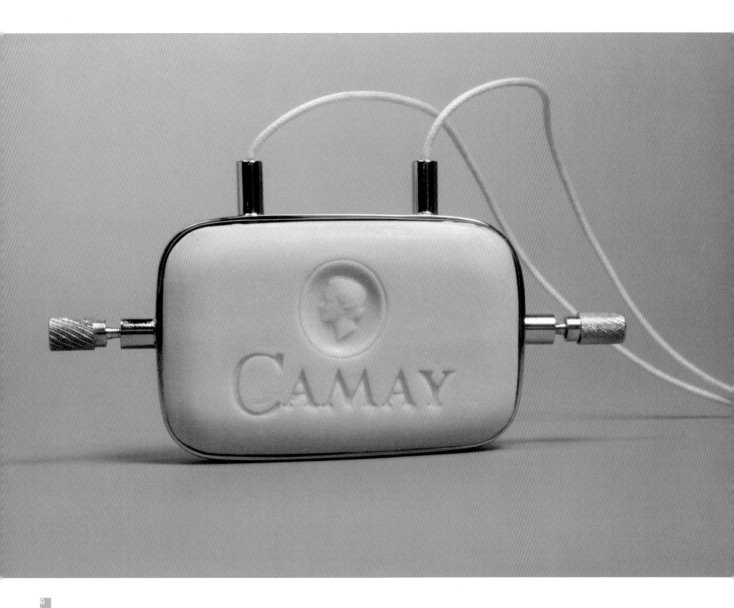

6. *Camay Necklace*
Soap, chromed silver,
cotton cord
5 x 4 cm
2005

1. *Rubber Stamp Bracelet*
Rubber stamp and ink
2005

ƏRTHUR HASH

Aesthetically unconventional, the work of Arthur Hash seeks to add to and extend the very definition of jewellery and to question the role and value of body adornment. Including unorthodox materials such as animal hair, cornflakes, cough drops, dust, pornography, and toilet paper, as well as coloured plastics and resins, Hash pushes design boundaries to their limits, experimenting with shape, size, wearability and conceptuality. Combining everyday ephemera in a myriad of complex geometrics, he highlights the value of time, memory and emotion, situating jewellery as an apparatus of commemoration and celebration and, at the same time, preserving the smaller events of his life in concrete form. Pleasing to the eye, his eclectically inspired and reinvented forms are difficult to place – each one stemming from the maker's experiences and emotions, unknown to the viewer. Formed from irregular juxtapositions, pieces elevate the ordinary, transforming the banal into something beautiful to behold. "Using everyday materials that I come into contact with comforts and enables me to take a little piece of home with me", explains Hash. "The materials that I use tend to be odd choices but making rings from dryer lint reminds me to do my laundry and rings made from cigarette butts remind me that I need to quit smoking. With the value and definition of jewellery constantly changing, I feel that personal inspiration is increasingly important and the right combination can produce new exotic materials that to me is more elegant and valuable than gold, silver or diamonds."

Technology, too, plays a central role in the development of Hash's work. Though pieces appear aesthetically organic, each is born from a complex process of technological experimentation during which the designer works upon multiple pieces collaboratively. "These days", Hash elaborates, "I sketch using a three-dimensional modelling programme enabling me to visualise each piece before it is made. During the construction process, the piece evolves and tends to move in one direction or the other depending on material and process – I consider most of my pieces works in progress."

2. *Silhouette Brooches*
Brooch installation
(380 pieces)
Mild steel, paint
2005

3. *Coffee Ring Brooch*
Copper and paint
2005

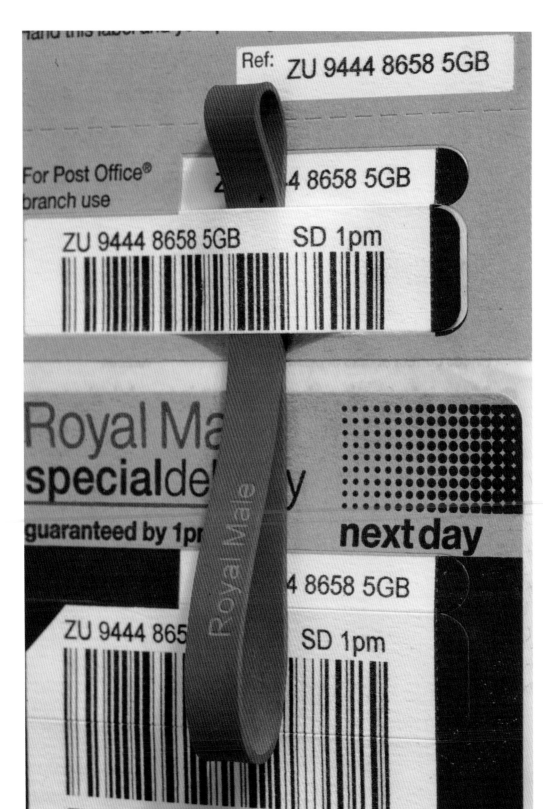

Ref: ZU 9444 8658 5GB

For Post Office®
branch use

ZU 9444 8658 5GB   SD 1pm

Royal Ma
specialde
guaranteed by 1p

next day

4 8658 5GB   SD 1pm

ZU 9444 865

1. *Royal Male*
Bracelet
Rubber band presented
on paper
2006

2. *Sizeable Rubber Bands*
Bracelets
Rubber, silver
2004

cRaig isAAc

Sometimes the simplest ideas can be the best – and Craig Isaac proves this point with his *Royal Male* series of bracelets. Taking direct inspiration from the rubber bands used to bind British Royal Mail packages of correspondence (bands that are sporadically left on unsuspecting doorsteps by postmen), Isaac has developed a colourful and inventive range of jewellery. By transforming refuse into the wearable, notions of disposal and re-invention are explored. As Isaac explains: "By hijacking and twisting the Royal Mail brand and applying it to my bands they immediately become a decorative item, with many references to their original use." Isaac points out that the moment the discarded postman's band is picked up and worn on the wrist, it immediately shifts form and function, becoming a piece of ornamentation rather than something functional or utilitarian.

Manipulating popular internet forums such as MySpace, eBay and YouTube, Isaac is spreading the word, attempting to win over audiences to his cause – which is to "Jog a response from all viewers, encouraging them to become wearers of the postman's band, constantly building the number of participants." Isaac's accessible jewellery is not only inspiring trans-continental communication, but is also connecting traditional forms of correspondence with the virtual. Along with this ongoing project, Isaac plans to release further items under his Royal Male banner, addressing similar observations.

1. *The Pink Lady with the Chicken Legs*
Brooch
Textile, plastic animal, plastic
9.5 x 5.5 cm
2004
Photography: Eddo Hartmann

Felieke van der Leest

Unexpectedly avant-garde, the work of Felieke van der Leest taps into the surreal world of childhood aesthetics, presenting itself as a plastic embodiment of natural and fantastical worlds. Pandering to innate and nostalgic human tendencies, Van der Leest employs a quirky family of found toyshop inhabitants, recreating peculiarly the kitsch, fairy-tale mysticism of childhood. Inspired by her own fascinations with the apparatus of youth, with nature and traditional craftsmanship, she remodels and manipulates cheerful ready-mades, transforming them into collections of inspired jewelleries: conceptual in nature and curious in form. Deconstructing, rejoining and redressing a range of cheap plastic animals, pieces are formed from an engagement with both childish thought and desire. Adorned with crocheted threads, giraffes, lions, rabbits and pussy cats – symbols of nature and of childhood – find themselves disembodied and reformed, transformed into a surreal version of their former selves. Like Alice's experiences of Wonderland, Van der Leest's designs are infused with the unusual. Drenched in acid colour, each piece has been carefully constructed via a process of crochet, knit and metalwork combining the plastic creatures with delicate viscose and metallic textile threads, as well as sterling silver, gold and an array of precious gemstones – embedded as sparking, questioning eyes.
As a pride of tiny lion cubs circle head to tail, clothed in cowboy hats and billowing collars, mutant white kittens are dressed in pink, ducks' feet brazenly protruding from their pretty beaded skirts. Van der Leest's designs combine animal and human worlds, adorning the body of their owners in a variety of ways. At once extraordinary and alluring, they push jewellery design into uncertain spheres of the unknown and uncanny.

2. *Magician Tiger Club & his*
5½ Little Rabbits
Necklace
Silver, plastic animal, textile
43 cm
2004
Photography:
Eddo Hartmann

3. *The Cowboy Lion Club*
Bracelet
Plastic animal, textile,
glass, gold
18 cm
2004
Photography:
Eddo Hartmann

4. *The Black Clown with the Golden Heart*
Brooch
Textile, plastic animal, polymer clay
17 x 10 cm
2005
Photography:
Eddo Hartmann

5. *Emperor Penguin Freddi with Polar Bear Claw*
Necklace object and ring for humans
Textile, plastic animal, gold, cubic zirconia
10 x 7 cm
2005
Photography:
Eddo Hartmann

Lindsey Mann

Checked, polka-dotted and multi-coloured, Lindsey Mann's playful and retro-inspired jewellery can't help but get noticed. Combining aluminium in an array of hues with silver, vintage plastics and other found materials, Mann employs a variety of engineering and jewellery techniques to create a range of sculptural and commercial brooches, neckpieces, rings and bangles. "My work crosses boundaries between jewellery design and sculpture, with inspiration derived from a fascination with old tin toys, interior decoration and general gadgetry." Taking cues from antique tin toys, Mann often incorporates simple kinetic elements such as coils to her pieces, "to add a sense of fun". Her *Layered Bangles*, featuring stripes, spots and myriad colours interestingly include fragments of vintage knitting needles in addition to aluminium.

Mann's work in anodised aluminium began when experimenting with printing and assembly techniques while studying jewellery design. She soon went on to develop a method of printing and dying which achieves a vibrant and bold effect. "Colour is very important to me", Mann points out, "so there is a range of pastels and vibrant tones featuring throughout my work. I am interested in simple shapes and the layering of pattern with which I create gloriously mismatched combinations."

1. *Getting To Know You*
Brooch
Printed aluminium, silver, steel pin
2004
Photography: Helen Gell

2. *Round Rings*
Anodised aluminium, vintage
plastics, silver
2005
Photography: Joe Low

3. *Propeller Necklace*
Printed aluminium,
silver, magnet, vintage
knitting needles
2004
Photography: Helen Gell

1. Three Brooches
Plastic, silver, steel
2004
Photography: Roger Casas

2. *Solitaire Brooch*
Silver, steel
2005

marc monzó

Challenging notions of symbolic versus economic value, Spanish jeweller Marc Monzó creates petite wearable objects from a variety of everyday and precious materials. "Since I was a young child", says Monzó, "I have been attracted to very small objects and jewellery allows me to work in this dimension." Featuring elegant forms and multicoloured rhinestones and plastics, Monzó's creations take direct inspiration from the 'solitaire' archetype, with a unique twist. Unlike the traditional model, many of Monzó's rings are either far too small to be worn as a ring, or are hugely oversized – able to envelope a wrist like a bracelet.

The almost faithful recreation of the solitaire takes on an altered meaning when worn in an entirely different manner – it is this kind of reinterpretation and inversion of traditional practices that makes Monzó's work so intriguing. Toying with perceptions, Monzó confuses insignificance and worth by employing a variety of opposing materials within a singular piece. Nearly every design includes materials that have been transformed – plastic objects are awarded a layer of silver through electroforming, while silver components are finished with lacquer. "Plastic is one of my favourite materials", explains Monzó; "it is warm, colourful, lightweight and resistant. I also work with traditional precious metals such as silver and gold, but like to give the same value to all materials whether banal or valuable."

3. *A Flat Surface*
Rings
Silver, rhodium, gold plated
silver
2006

4. Pin
Ping pong ball, silver
2003

2. *frrrr* (detail)
Object
Ready-made clock, sewing
machine parts, steel cable
70 cm
2002

3. *frrrr* (detail)
Object
Ready-made clock, sewing
machine parts, steel cable
70 cm
2002

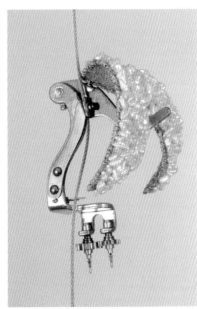

NOA NaDiR

1. *frrrr* (detail)
Object
Ready-made clock, sewing
machine parts, steel cable
70 cm
2002

To create her idiosyncratic and elaborate jewellery, Noa Nadir utilises the tradition of gold crafting as a means of self-expression. Telling a story and illustrating personal experiences through her designs is of utmost importance to Nadir, who views her practice as "a personal dialogue with the world". Slotting somewhere between ornament and accessory, her striking pieces can either adorn a body or complement a space. The distinctive and multi-faceted piece *frrrr* is a perfect example of her work: part sculpture, part jewellery. What looks like the inner workings of clocks and more organic inspirations like butterflies are combined and slung along gold wire – equally at home as an arresting accessory or as an art object. "I aspire for a wider definition of the term jewellery", she explains, "aiming to diverge from practicality and to sometimes leave the natural habitat of the jewellery – the body."

Nadir's intricate, mechanically informed pieces involve used and antique materials; they are a fusion of unusual bits and pieces that impart a history and sense of nostalgia with the accompanying contemporary materials and design. While Nadir views herself as a contemporary goldsmith and practises established techniques, as an artist she is inspired to depart from the conventional. Nadir believes she has "developed a liberated and relevant language, loyal to values of design, beauty and aesthetics, while preserving old techniques alongside new technology. By walking this path, I take part in a broad cultural and artistic dialogue."

4. *rrrring*
Ring
Ready-made clock, sewing
machine parts, rubber bands
10 x 5 x 5 cm
2005

5. *fffly* (detail)
Object
Ready-made clock, sewing
machine parts, steel cable
50 cm
2004

Ted Noten

Situating itself happily between product design and art, the work of Ted Noten extends definitions of jewellery, bringing together multiple artistic disciplines, and challenging various design precepts and conventions. Perhaps best known for the interactive work *Chew Your Own Brooch* – where individuals were invited to chew gum into a satisfactory shape then to be cast in gold or silver and thus transformed into a wearable piece of jewellery – Noten has been persistent in his search for an alternative vocabulary and aesthetic. Having collaborated with other artists and with design companies such as the Dutch collective Droog Design, he is recognised as one of the most innovative jewellery designers working in The Netherlands today. His avant-garde works present themselves as separate sculptural pieces, as *objets d'art* or contemporary curiosities, steeped in freshly prescribed symbolism and rich in allegory and allusion – works that, with a certain tongue-in-cheek humour, take everyday items and drop them into a variety of uncanny contexts. As Gert Staal of The Netherlands Design Institute puts it, in looking for "fixed meaning in the banal and cultivated, he debunks their essence, then reinvents them back into reality [and] in affecting and infecting symbolic values he actually reveals their unmistakable intangibility".

Searching for meaning within the everyday object or image, Noten relinquishes and then redefines significance, infusing each one with a new life and purpose. Through the reinterpretation of household items, he elevates the commonplace, securing it as aesthetically and symbolically valuable. Often minimal in appearance, pieces combine precious metals (gold and sterling silver) with found objects, to evoke a sense of familiarity and eclecticism. Readymade monotone shoes are fitted with 24 carat gold innersoles; women's handbags are reconstructed and transformed. Made of transparent acrylic, they encase hybrid collections: a golden gun, an ice pick, an engraved bullet and a goose egg each sit suspended in plastic. These works appear as embodiments of the obscure, designed as both a critique of modern life and as a means of defying the conventions of both jewellery and society; they refute the socially determined perceptions and definitions of acceptability, extending to a wider design context to embrace architecture, art, fashion and politics.

1. *My Last Cigarette*
Brooch
24ct gold
2000

2. Saint James Cross Revisited
Brooch
See: www.stjamescrossrevisited

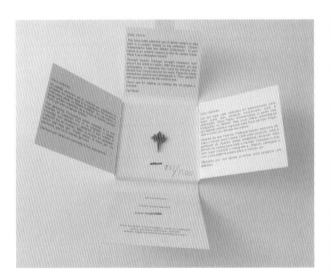

Welcome to the St. James Cross Revisited website. This is an art project initiated by Ted Noten. You can read about the project and participate if you like.

Through history Portugal brought treasures from around the world to Lisbon. Nowadays, a big deal of these treasures are part of the beautiful collection of the Museu Nacional de Arte Antiga. People from all over the world come to Lisbon to admire these art treasures.

With this in mind, Ted Noten imagined a way of reversing this flow. He designed a brooch by literally separating the little red espada which originally is situated in the Insignia of St. James. During the summer of 2005, every seventh visitor to the museum receives a brooch. Then they are asked, as they go back home, to make a picture or a portrait with the brooch in their hometown. Finally, they are invited to place their photo in this site.

The result, to be seen in the photo gallery, pretends to be a very diverse register of this brooches' migration. If you want to upload your photo, please log in. Information over the old espada and the new one you can find in the history, and if you would like to participate but do not have a brooch, please visit the shop in the website.

Thanks for visiting.

name   Angelica

story   Here am I in my favorite place in amsterdam
           for this summer: my balcony!

continent Europe

country

city

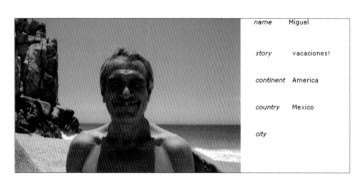

name   Miguel

story   vacaciones!

continent America

country   Mexico

city

3. *New Tiara for Maxima*
Helmet, chromed
2004

4. *Lady-K*
Bag, engraved gun
and bullet gold plated,
textile
2005

ARTWORKS AND OBJECTS

An Alleweireldt

Iris Bodemer

Silke Fleischer

Dongchun Lee

Carla Nuis

Lucy Sarneel

Karin Seufert

Catherine Truman

Lisa Walker

Annamaria Zanella

AN ALLEWEIRELDT

Perennially inspired by the detritus of everyday life, An Alleweireldt's refreshingly clever and quirky jewellery transforms the seemingly worthless into precious, wearable objects. Alleweireldt's recent series of jewellery focuses on the theme of opposites, presenting familiar and often discarded matter in a new context, where a balance is struck between common materials and precious metal and stones.

By working with generic material, Alleweireldt is also re-evaluating notions of value and worth. She notes, "We tend to underestimate the beauty of that which is outwardly humble or common. Value is subjective; every single piece of material around us offers a unique beauty, it is there for us to explore and discover." Employing diverse refuse such as ice-cream sticks, old records and buttons, alongside the more traditional material of gold and silver, Alleweireldt's pieces do just that – explore the beauty of the overlooked and forgotten. The *Ice-cream Stick Necklace* and *Fan Earrings* feature an inventive re-working of a base fabric – successfully crafted into stylish accessories. With *Diskette Bracelet*, pieces of a record have been modified to form semi-circular, fan-like discs that are joined to create a unique bracelet, with hints of crimson adding to the dramatic effect. Alleweireldt not only manages to transform the fabric of an old record into a chic, wearable object through her considerable design finesse and technical ability, but also reveals the surprising beauty of an ostensibly disposable item.

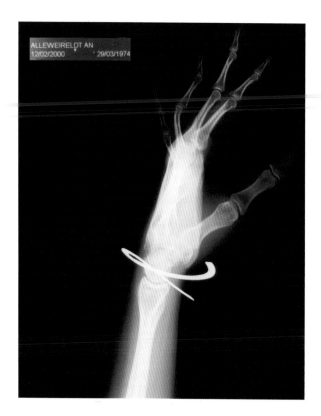

1. *Bangle in 2-D*
Silver, own hand, x-ray
8 x 8 cm
1999
Photography:
Doctor Johan Florizoone

2. *Diskette Bracelet*
Old diskette, cotton
10 x 20 cm
2006
Photography: EMS photo

iris Bodemer

"I always make my jewellery like I'm drawing", says Iris Bodemer; "I like to draw my ideas and emotions directly into the material." Her pieces tell stories, "what I'm wondering about", as she puts it. Her most recent series of rings was inspired by a family heirloom, a ring that had belonged to her great-great-grandfather; when he died, his widow wrapped it in wool so that she could wear it. Bodemer, then, invests her own work with this very personal inherited memory, changing the size and fit of the pieces in the same way, so that these fragments of coral, pearl, and other semi-precious stones seem to be bound to the ring by the knotted, wound wool. There is also, here, an intimation of a more common narrative, the notion of tying thread about the finger so as not to forget.

She is interested in "still lifes and rebus", placing apparently disparate objects alongside each other, suggesting connections to be found through emotion and fantasy. These seemingly arbitrary combinations of crafted pieces with found objects, beautifully presented, take on an intrigue, inviting the viewer to contemplate their meaning, to join Bodemer in "finding the right expression".

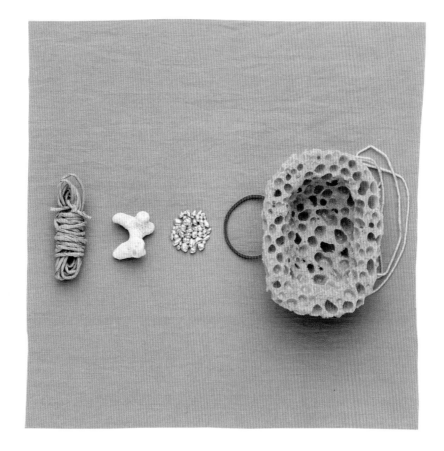

1. Rings
Silver, bronze, stones, wool,
raffia
Approx. 4 x 2.5 x 1 cm each
2004
Photography: Julian Kirschler

2. Neckpiece
Fine gold, coral, serpentine,
sponge, string, rubber, textile
19 x 19 x 3 cm
2004
Photography: Julian Kirschler

silke fleischer

Trained in the arts of silversmithing and ceramics, Silke Fleischer has adopted an unusual approach to jewellery design, bringing together the two disciplines to create a body of work highly evocative in its aesthetic. Establishing her pieces as part of a wider investigation into aspects of corporality and functionality, Fleischer's work seeks to uncover complex relationships existing between the everyday object and human form. She attempts to explore, through a process of investigation and experimentation, shapes that make use of the space around us – both actively and passively. Objects such as the cup and the ring, "deemed insurmountably connected to the body", serve as inspiration for Fleischer's work. Embarking upon an exploration into the different ways in which such items can be juxtaposed with the human form she views her work as a type of research – an intuitive, creative research concerning the relationship between design and art, the body and the object: as a means of individual, artistic and social exploration. Pieces are rendered in smooth, simple forms that combine sterling silver with simple white ceramic shapes, overtly reflective of the everyday. Rejecting colour, they are clean and minimalist in appearance yet heavy in symbolism, meaning and metaphor. Fleischer's jewellery often takes on the form of two-dimensional cut-outs, flattened into interlinking silver chains, appearing as compressed objects transformed: as small wearable sculptures, ambiguous but beautiful.

3. *Drops*
Ring
Silver 2006

4. *Somewhere in Between*
Bracelet/bowl
Silver plated
2006

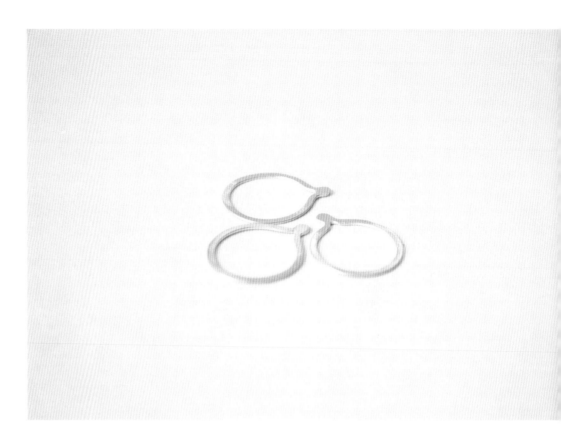

5. *Drops*
Chain
Silver
2006

Dongchun Lee

Petite embodiments of personal thought, emotion, feeling and perception, the jewellery of Dongchun Lee has been conceived as a form of self-expression and as a means of communication with the wearer or viewer. Understated yet evocative, brooches and pendants appear as delicate two-dimensional sketches, bringing closer the fields of art and design. Female bodies sit and stand, outlined, twisted and contorted within the circular frames in which they pose. Their breasts, thighs and arms, rendered expressively in sweeping movements, are truncated by the very designs that define them. While some are clearly recognisable as human forms, others are less tangible, expertly concealed in shape and form. Each one executed in a palette of greys and black, pieces are formed from iron – a material chosen specifically for its inconvenience to jewellery design. Though it symbolises both power and strength, iron is not durable, slowly weathering, rusting and decaying – representing for the maker the passing of time, emotion and thought. Fascinated by the body, simultaneously familiar and mysterious, Lee seeks to explore notions of transformation. Working with the human form as a starting point, he creates new perceptions and fresh, undefined forms, each one expressing something personal to the maker himself. Tapping into the complexities of relationships and experiences, Lee's works draw from his own subconscious, pinpointing and selecting fragmentary feelings to be expressed through the appropriate design. Via a process of self-exploration, emotions surface, "exposed as unrefined, unfiltered forms on a blank sheet". Translated into jewellery designs, these become a way of better understanding the human unconscious, our fears, desires and dreams. Lee explains: "Modern jewellery requires exchanges of emotional and sometimes intellectual thoughts – between the artists and the wearer. I attempt to embody my abstract emotion, feeling and unrecognised self-image to find my identity and configure myself into something sensual through jewellery."

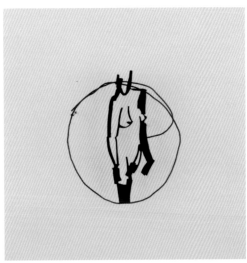

1. *Draw Pendant*
Iron
6.5 x 9.7 x 0.5 cm
2004

2. *Draw Brooch*
Iron
8.2 x 9.2 x 0.5 cm
2004

3. *Draw Pendant*
Iron
11 x 13 x 0.3 cm
2004

4. *Draw Pendant*
Iron, painting
8 x 11 x 1.6 cm
2004

CarLA NUIS

1. *Potato*
Object/brooch
Silver sheet, 0.15 mm, copper
sheet, 0.15 mm
4 x 7 cm
2004

2. *Pearl Necklace Bronzino*
Necklace
Silver sheet, 0.15 mm
28 2 cm spheres, 70 cm total
length
2005
Photography: Eddy Wenting

"For as long as I can remember I have had a passion for patterns", reveals Carla Nuis, and glancing over her intricate gold, silver and bronze designs this is immediately evident. The elaborate nature of Nuis' jewellery suggests the historic tradition of filigree – the ornamental working of fine wire (typically gold or silver) into a delicate tracery. But beneath the detailed surface of her designs is a contrasting conceptual framework. "My approach breaks with the traditional idea of ornamentation being a supplementary matter", Nuis explains of her elegant designs. "Instead, I seek to enhance the grandeur of the jewellery by transforming the patterns into open worked three-dimensional jewellery objects."

While Nuis' work may have an antiquated appearance superficially, they are actually the product of complex computer aided methods, chemical and electrolytic etching techniques, forging and laser welding. Through these various techniques her patterns are mapped onto thin gold or silver sheets and moulded into three-dimensional egg-shaped objects. She is inspired by a range of material, from organic matter like potatoes and pearls through to fine art. One example of Nuis' work, *Pearl Necklace Bronzino*, references a Renaissance painting by Agnolo Bronzino from 1545; taking on the appearance of a string of pearls but crafted out of silver, the piece alludes to the pomegranate textile print dress and pearl necklace adorning the painting's subject. Nuis aimed to capture and reinterpret these two parts of the painting to form one object, "a perfect symbiosis of optimal beauty between the rich patterned velvet and subtle lustre of the pearls".

3. *Sphere 1*
Brooch/object
Silver sheet, 0.15 mm
4 cm ø
2004

4

4. *Pendant Brooch*
Brooch
9ct yellow gold sheet, 0.12 mm
5 x 9 x 0.7 cm
2005
Photography: Eddy Wenting

Lucy Sarneel

Inspiration comes in many forms for Lucy Sarneel, whose jewellery exhibits an innovative meld of numerous influences, materials and hand crafting techniques. A constant source of creative stimulation for Sarneel is, quite simply, everyday life experience, and the passing of time; she explains: "We all try to deal with notions of time such as our personal lifetime, historic time and universal time. With my jewellery, I try to express these factors." One way in which Sarneel's jewellery connotes a sense of chronology is in her employment of used materials, where the fabric of a once functional item is reworked and given new life as a decorative object. Alongside used materials, Sarneel also presents precious stones, another form of inspiration to her. "One assimilates power from a jewel by wearing it and at the same time one adds power and meaning to it; this imaginary 'breathing in and out' of a jewel fascinates me."

Her delicate, azure and steely-grey hued necklace, *Lola*, encapsulates this juxtaposition of precious materials against rudimentary items. Materials used include gold, zinc, silk string and wood – the wooden component being the cast off handle of an old washing up brush that bears the trademark name 'Lola'. Highlighting the 'naturalness' of particular materials as well as redefining and clarifying what is perceived as 'valuable' is intrinsic to Sarneel's practice, as she describes it: "Through handcraftsmanship I transform everyday materials into precious objects."

1. *Lola*
Necklace
Zinc, silk string, gold, wood
(old washing-up brush,
trade mark 'Lola')
14 cm
2004

2. *Lola* (detail)

karin seufert

As the conception of jewellery extends to embrace a wider version of what is perceived to be wearable or acceptable, Karin Seufert seeks to discover a new language of expression, opening up definitions and embracing new materials and forms. Dismissing limitations, she upholds the view that jewellery can in fact be made from anything – from the mundane and everyday to the surreal and obscure. The significance of her chosen materials take a central role in the development of her designs, stemming from an engagement with narrative, memory and meaning – their previous usage and history enriching each individual piece. Seufert arranges found materials in new settings, fascinated by the sense of alienation that arises from the act of placing an object in an unfamiliar context, tapping into both their history and the new, contemporary environment in which they have been positioned. Strongly influenced by her immediate, everyday surroundings, Seufert seeks out colour combinations, shapes, objects, materials and patterns, building a reservoir of ideas to be called upon when conceiving her next design.

The materials available to such an approach offer limitless possibilities, combinations and formations. PVC is a favourite, serving as a futuristic skin or means of encasement, transforming existing objects into quirky, innovative jewelleries. Small items found on the streets, in shops or in flea markets form the base material for her work, serving as fragments of memory and of reality to be utilised in new ways and forms. Combined with sterling silver, buttons, thread, rubber, china and enamel, simple and complex shapes are created, designed to be pinned to and hung from the body in a variety of ways. With textures kept smooth and simple, colours are bold and basic, often monotone. These minimalist pieces are muted in form, understated yet loaded, rich in association and symbolism.

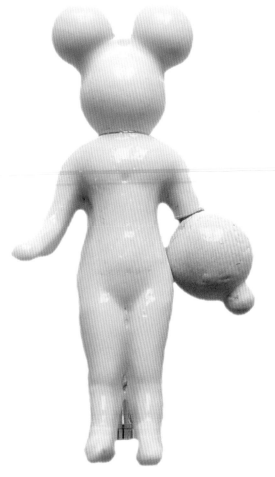

1

1. Brooch
China, polyurethane, colorit,
remanium
7 x 3.8 cm
2005

2. Brooch
China, silver, colorit, enamel
6 x 3.5 cm
2004

3. Necklace
PVC, thread, press-button
11.5 x 30 cm
2005

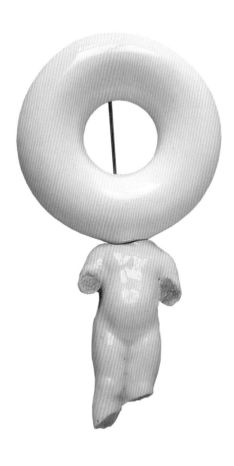

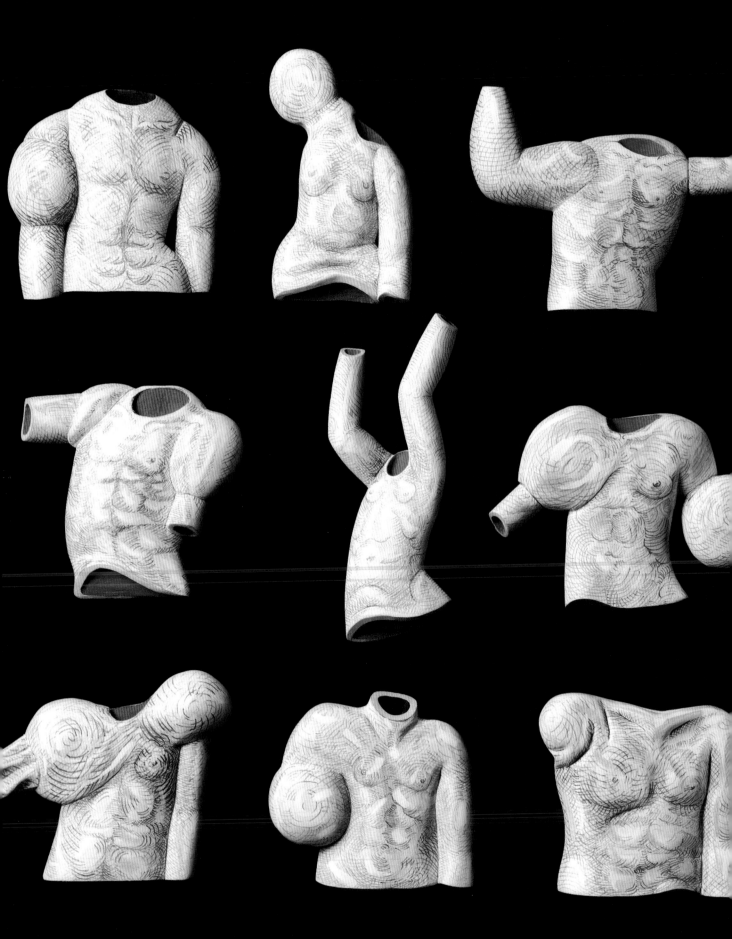

1. *Fugitive Anatomies*
Brooch series
Carved lime wood, paint,
graphite
10 cm
2005

2. *Black Drape Brooches*
Carved lime wood,
paint, graphite
10 cm
2005

CATherine TRUMAN

With figurative and sculptural elements at the fore of her most recent designs, Catherine Truman emphasises the inherent art in jewellery design. Her current interests surround the ways in which human anatomy is translated through artistic process and scientific method; she notes "how the experience of living inside a body has been given meaning". Truman points out that "the interior of the body is a concealed territory – the less we see the more we imagine. I'm interested in how we reveal and conceal the unfamiliar – the unaccustomed, the invisible."

Hand carved from English lime wood and embellished with paint and graphite, her *Fugitive Anatomies* series of brooches aim to evoke, Truman says, sensory responses of physical recognition through their resemblance to the human body. Although representative of human torsos, the hollow interiors and cloth-like draping give the appearance of the torso being just a garment, an outer shell. Highlighting the mysterious nature of that which is concealed, Truman's *Black Drape Brooches* appear to be a single curtain loosely tied, almost revealing what is beneath, perhaps alluding to the body upon which they are pinned.

1. Work table pieces that may
become jewellery
Various materials
2005

2. Brooch
Gold, plastic, glue
3 x 1 cm
2005

lisa walker

"What initially did not appear in the slightest to be 'jewellery
as we know it' is, all of a sudden, precious and becoming."
Otto Künzli on Lisa Walker

Lisa Walker has a knack for turning junk into jewellery. Whether it's a basic
household item, quirky finds from a hobby-shop or remnants from the
studio floor, her magic touch can transform the most banal objects into
eye-catching accessories. Bypassing traditional goldsmith practices, Walker's
jewellery takes its form through an idiosyncratic mix of gluing, cutting,
bending, stuffing, embroidering, crafting and rolling – and all from an
endless array of unusual materials. While Walker is unquestionably prolific,
she's certainly no perfectionist: "I'm not really a very good sewer, or solderer,
or gluer, or goldsmith", she reveals. "In fact I'm not really a technical expert
at anything" – and therein lies the charm of her work. Much of the appeal
of Walker's jewellery lies in its unashamedly amateur appearance – clumps of
plastic, metal and even actual rubbish constitute her designs. Despite Walker's
unorthodox methods, materials and experimental approach to making,
there is an apparent respect for the art of jewellery design where the typical
aesthetics and dimensions of jewellery are consistently maintained. In an
expressionist manner, Walker believes that it is the creative process itself, and
not always the end result, that is crucial to her work.

'Jewellery' is a term loosely applied to her inimitable designs; these
are objects that are more aptly described as bite-size pieces of art that can (if
desired) be worn. "I want to make pieces that don't fit any jewellery recipes",
Walker explains of her eccentric designs, "yet still make sense as jewellery.
This is really making jewellery, this is really falling slap, bang into it, but in
my own way that I still find exciting."

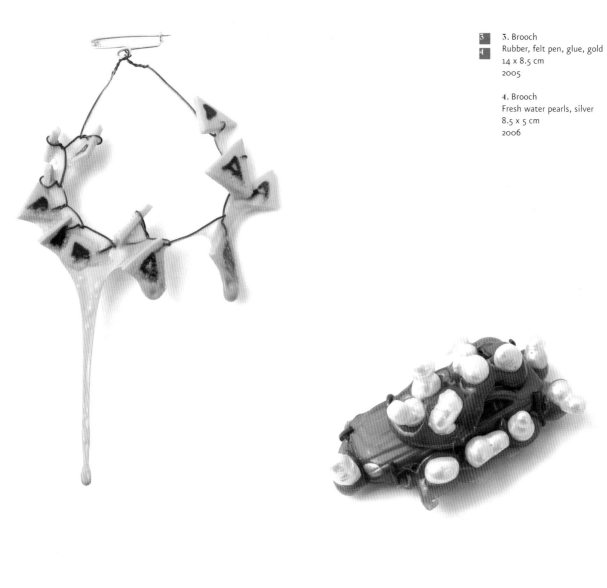

3. Brooch
Rubber, felt pen, glue, gold
14 x 8.5 cm
2005

4. Brooch
Fresh water pearls, silver
8.5 x 5 cm
2006

5. Brooch
Rubbish from workshop floor
10 cm ø
2006

annamaria zanella

Highly expressive in appearance, the works of Annamaria Zanella break through the boundaries of jewellery design to embrace the characteristics of sculpture and fine art. Informed by the precepts of Art Povera (an artistic discipline seeking to dissolve preconceived divisions between 'rich' and 'poor' materials), Zanella explores concepts of 'poverty' and 'the poor', combining pieces of rusty iron and broken glass with precious and semi-precious metals. Colours are kept bold and basic, while forms remain minimal yet striking, understated yet provocative. Silver, enamels, glass, gold, copper, resins, plastics and paints are moulded and transformed, resulting in aesthetic juxtapositions of manipulated shape and form. Surfaces are corroded, rough and textured, built up in layers and enlivened by pigments of vibrant colour and gold. Treated and reformed through oxidisation and the application of acids, enamels and pigments, humble materials are thus elevated and rich ones humbled, taking on new meanings as they morph from their original form. Blending the plastic and pictorial, each piece is born from a different constructive arrangement, inspired by anything from the architectural to the organic. The details of the everyday — of doors, windows, roofs and rooms — are combined with the world of human biology, with nature and the natural environment. Drawing upon personal experience and emotion, these works tap into the autobiographical, experimenting with forms of psychological and introspective analysis. Like miniature works of art, they stand as sculptural expressions of life and memory.

1. *Containers*
Brooch
Silver, gold, enamel,
oxidation
7 x 5.5 x 3 cm
2005
Photography: F Storti

2. *Marte*
Brooch
Silver, gold acrylic
composite, gold powder,
enamel, paint
10 x 8.5 x 1.3 cm
2006
Photography: L Trento,
G Rustichelli

1. *Blue Cell*
Brooch
Papier-mâché, silver,
gold, acrylics
2003
Photography: F Neumuller

2. *Bionic Heart*
Brooch
Silver, gold, enamel,
oxidations, acrylics
7 x 5.5 x 3 cm
2005
Photography: F Storti

3. *Room*
Brooch
Gold, iron
6.5 x 5 x 2 cm
2001
Photography: L Trento

LAYERS OF ADORNMENT

dinie besems
monika brugger
madeleine furness
rheanna lingham
husam el odeh
tiffany parbs
salima thakker

1. *Mat Necklace*
Silver
30 x 30 cm
2001
Photography:
Bettina Neumann

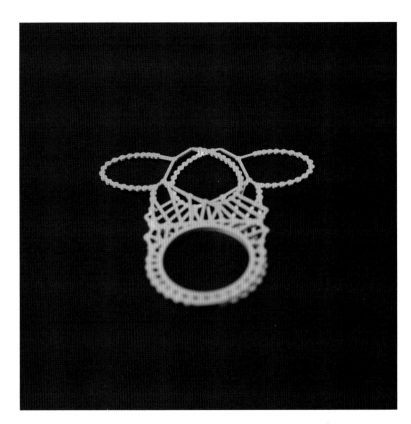

2. Ring
Laser-cut steel
2006
Photography:
Bettina Neuman

diNiε bεsεms

Conceptually focused jeweller Dinie Besems has of late been preoccupied with the seemingly contrary notion of 'meaninglessness' for her designs. As it turns out, it's not such an easy task – but with a machine-made computer tool at her disposal dictating shapes for her, Besems has been attempting to construct wearable designs that concentrate on surface over substance. Inspired by such varying and abstract subjects as "nature-experience and mathematics", Besems frequently uses silver to craft primarily classic items including necklaces, brooches and rings.

Specifically utilising complex principles within the field of 'Computational Geometry', via a program developed for her by a graphic designer, Besems' "dream was to create beauty through a mathematical formula that would shape my ideas for me". Besems' captivating jewellery finds a meeting point between the strict, precise characteristics of mathematics and the unrestricted freedom of the natural environment. Her rings feature an unusual fusion of angular forms, softened through the recurrent inclusion of organic circular shapes. While the result should be 'meaningless', Besems' artistic process begins and ends with a firm conceptual basis. "The most important thing is generating and constructing ideas, working them together until there is a strong concept that makes sense."

3. *Private Assignment*
Ring
Silver plated brass
2006

4. *DV7/250*
Brooches
Plastic, paper
5 x 5 cm each
2006

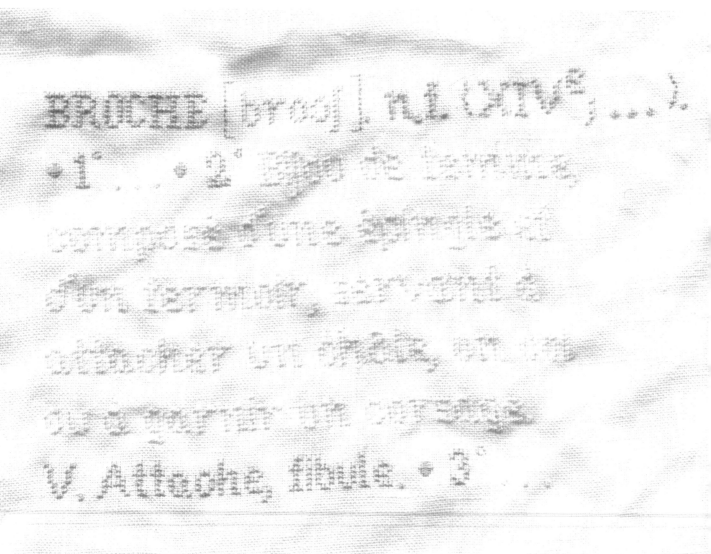

BROCHE [bʀɔʃ] n.f. (XIIᵉ ; ...).
• 1°... • 2° Bijou de fantaisie composé d'une épingle et d'un fermoir, servant à attacher un châle, un vêtement ou ajouté un corsage. V. Attache, fibule. • 3°...

Petit Robert 1

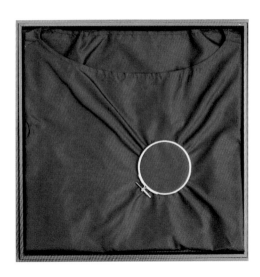

MONiKA BrUGGer

The inherent relationship between jewellery and clothing is an obvious one; a piece of jewellery is chosen to complement an outfit, to complete a look; and the two aspects of adornment must be compatible. A heavy brooch will pull a silk blouse out of shape; a necklace must suit a neckline; a bangle shouldn't interfere with a cuff. The two have much in common besides: a sense of tactility, the need for a comfortable fit, the means of portraying an identity or making a statement. The scope for symbolism is perhaps even greater for jewellery than it is for clothing; if an outfit can make a broad statement about taste, social class, nationality, then a piece of jewellery can say something very specific to the individual, about personal associations, inheritance, and memory.

Monika Brugger's work is preoccupied with "the situation of the jewel in society", and the relationship between people and what they wear. Exploring the notion of memory, she projects the ghost of a daisy chain on the neck of a wearer – a residue of childhood play left upon the body, luminous and intangible, yet more constant than the object it recalls, long since shrivelled and lost. Similarly, a cherry earring evokes the imagery of childhood, the simple forms and friendly, bold colours, appealing to a common reservoir of familiar but forgotten things.

Brugger is interested in "the engagement between jewel and clothing in contact with the human body", in the intimacy of what is worn against the skin. She engages particularly with notions of femininity, and her use of embroidery and sewing is a reference to what she calls "female work", made in the home. Shirts are stitched with the shape of a missing brooch, or with a dictionary definition of 'brooch'; others, sun-bleached, are left with a dark patch where a jewel once was, like the trace of a picture removed from a wall. Elsewhere, a hole burned through the fabric of a garment occupies the place that a piece of jewellery might otherwise be, as if the piece has somehow burned its way through to the skin. The clothes themselves seem imbued with the memory of what was worn upon them.

1. *Inseparable*
Blouse with embroidered
brooch
Linen, silk thread
Brooch 8.7 x 10 cm
2002
Photography: François
Seigneur, Arles

2. *Little Black Dress*
Dress, tambour, wooden box
Silk, taffeta, wood,
silver, iron
Tambour 8.77 cm ø
Box 38.2 x 38.2 cm
2001
Photography: François
Seigneur, Arles

3 4

3. *Mark* (detail)
Photography: Corinne Janier,
Arles

4. *Women*
Installation
(from left to right)
Red
Embroidered dress
Starched cotton, silk thread
Dress 132 cm
Embroidery 5 x 4.8 cm

Mark
Dress
Cotton/linen
Dress 134 cm
Hole 8 cm ø

Soleil
Dress
Cotton
Dress 129 cm
'Sun' detail 8.3 cm ø
2001
Photography: Corinne Janier,
Arles

These works question the boundary between jewellery and clothing, so that the two incorporate each other; the shirt becomes a function of the piece, rather than the jewellery serving only as an adornment. Indeed, the jewellery itself is made manifest in an absence – a hole, a stain, a faded patch – but the purpose of the garment itself is to provide a vehicle through which to make that absence apparent. In a similar inversion, her *Little Black Dress*, 2001, is a brooch pinned to a dress in such a way that it gathers surplus fabric, becoming an essential part of a garment which, unless worn with the piece, is hopelessly lopsided. Rather than an afterthought, added to an outfit as a final flourish, the work is an integral part of an outfit designed around it.

Brugger's work, then, brings to the fore some interesting questions surrounding the layers with which we choose to adorn ourselves, and the ways in which those layers interact. While jewellery does not have the aspect of necessity that clothing, at least at its most fundamental level, has, it is at the same time a potentially more durable possession, something that will last, be worn for a lifetime, passed on to successive generations. And it can carry associations that allow it to signify to the wearer something more personal and resonant than the more generic implications of the choice of clothing. By exploring the very notion of durability, through pieces which are at once made up of that which endures – memory – and at the same time are actually things lost or once forgotten, made manifest, Brugger examines the at times complex relationship that we have with the things we choose to wear, and the ways that we remember.

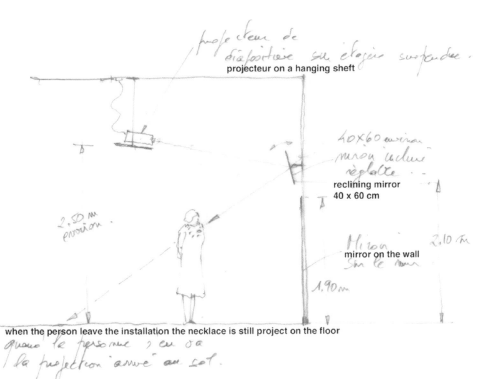

projecteur de
diapositive sur étagère suspendue.
projecteur on a hanging sheft

40 x 60 environ
miroir incliné
réglable
reclining mirror
40 x 60 cm

2,50 m
environ

Miroir
sur le mur
mirror on the wall

2,10 m

1,90 m

when the person leave the installation the necklace is still project on the floor
quand la personne s'en va
la projection arrive au sol.

4. *Jeuje*
Installation
Slide, projector, mirror
1999–2000
Technical sketch: François
Seigneur

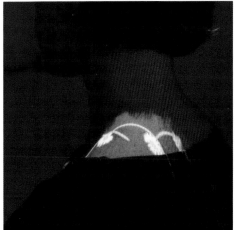

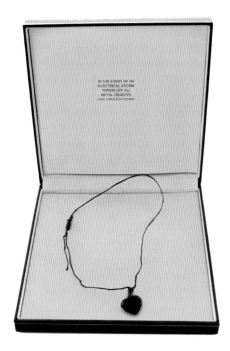

maɒeʟeiɴe ꜰuʀɴess

Official guidelines for behaviour in the event of an electrical storm recommend 'throwing off all metal objects and crouching down'. Madeleine Furness's rubber coated *Lightning Safe* jewellery offers a safeguard for the wearer caught out by lightning. This "paranoid, obsessive response" was inspired by the ghosts of necklaces, zippers, rivets and rings, branded on the skin of lightning strike victims. Furness collects documentation of these incidents, and has compiled a surprisingly extensive photographic archive of the phenomenon.

She collects, too, second-hand, broken jewellery; seemingly innocuous chains, lockets, and simple hoop earrings, a potential threat to the lightning strike-prone wearer, are rendered 'harmless' by a plastic coating. They have an association with an ancient and lasting function of jewellery; like the rabbit's foot, the St Christopher, the crucifix, they serve as amulets. Drawing upon and inverting this idea of jewellery as a means of protection against malign forces, Furness suggests that the piece is the source of the very danger it protects against, were it not for its 'lightning safe' layer. The experience she evokes is embodied in the jewellery itself; the same insulation that protects the skin makes the object appear blackened and burnt. The plastic covers the details of engravings, clogs the links of chains, disguising the original work and lending a unique appearance that simultaneously masks that which was unique to the original piece. The original pieces can only be imagined through the layers – do we know what is inside? are we right? Furness is perhaps, in this, issuing a challenge to more ubiquitous pieces (the very ones that might scar the wearer) making us look more closely at the ways in which layers – or metal plating, of tarnish or dirt, of meaning – are acquired.

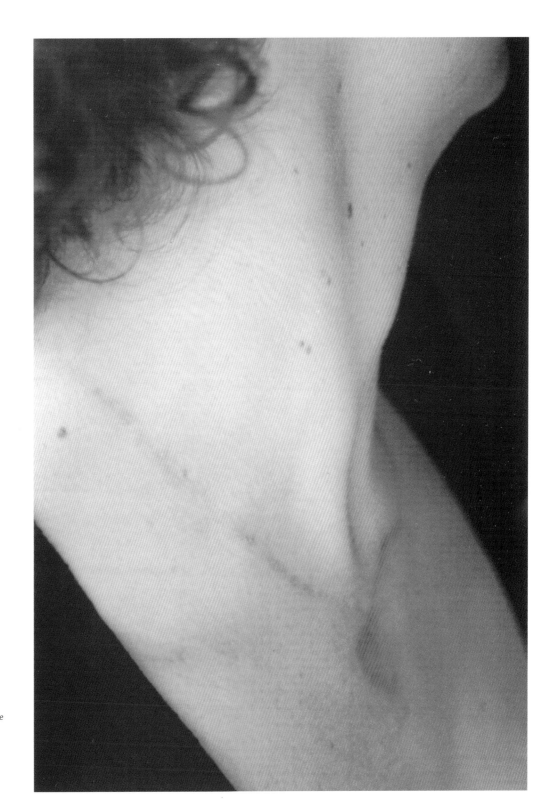

1. *'Lightning Safe' Locket*
Necklace and custom box
Silver, plastidip synthetic
rubber, magnets, box, dyes
Box 20 x 20 x 20 cm
2004
Photography: R Turner

2. *Lightning 'injury' – Necklace*
Framed colour photograph
Photograph, plastidip
synthetic rubber, aluminium
frame
31 x 41 cm
2002

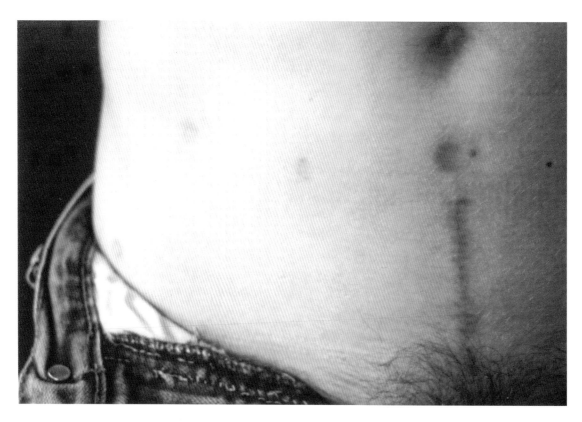

3. *Lightning 'injury' – Fly burn*
Framed colour photograph
Photograph, plastidip
synthetic rubber, aluminium
frame
31 x 41 cm
2002

Madeleine Furness's work in jewellery, fine art, and craft seeks to offer "real solutions to unreal problems". Inventive, wry, and intelligent, she addresses the relationship between people and objects; the ways in which objects are invested with symbolic value and superstitions, the stories they tell. These pieces provoke an active response, a sense of wonder that an ordinary piece of high street jewellery might become branded into your skin. But even without prior knowledge of the lightning story, these pieces, simultaneously recognisable and strange, have an aesthetic value and a wearability that belies their strongly conceptual origin.

These works are also indicative of a trend common to a number of contemporary makers who are utilising existing jewellery, posing the question "why bring more things into the world?" This approach conflates two poles in current jewellery production; on the one hand, the bespoke item, more usually individually crafted from precious materials, and on the other, the mass-market accessibility (and disposability) of the high street, which is flooded with machine-made versions of time honoured forms of jewellery. Designers are not credited here, and pieces have long since lost any specific reference to the originals; in Furness's work, the original pieces might equally be mass-produced or antique, but all receive the same treatment and are reinvented in her hands. Perhaps this reflects the current fashion climate, in which the boundaries between what endures and what passes, between *haute couture* and high street, are increasingly blurred.

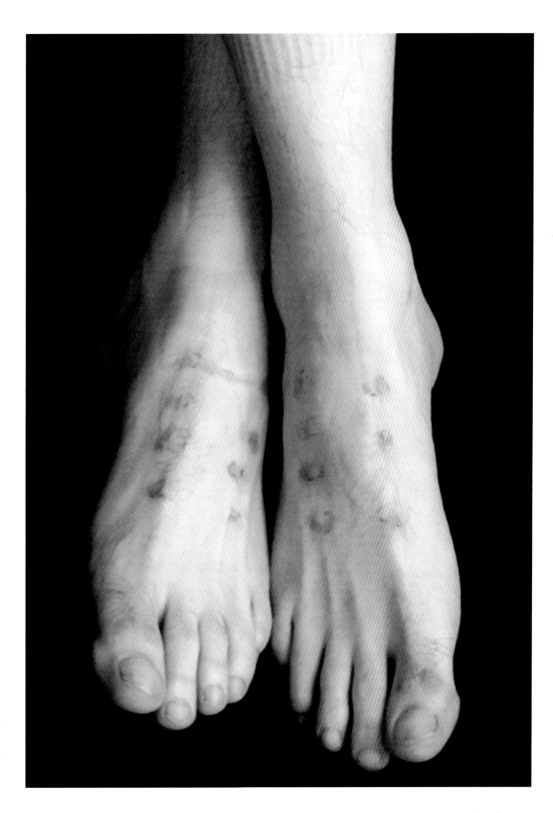

4. *Lightning 'injury' – Rivets*
Framed colour photograph
Photograph, plastidip
synthetic rubber, aluminium
frame
31 x 41 cm
2005

Rheanna Lingham

The work of Rheanna Lingham displays an intense engagement with the extravagant fashions of the late nineteenth century, playing out a baroque theatre of excess and decay and presenting itself as an embodiment of the horror and eroticism characteristic of that period. Inspired by symbols of decadence, from the crumbling Georgian house to birds, mourning jewellery and the Indian Maharaja, Lingham brings together expressive materials, handcrafting each piece to exacting standards. Plumes of lightweight feathers are combined with acrylics, metals, glass beads and ribbon, rich in exquisite detail and complex surface texture. Embracing the body, pieces are executed in a range of muted colours: in black, deep reds, greys and petrol blue. They blend expressive combinations of contrasting materials, bringing together the natural and manmade in a fusion of theatrical and sculptural forms.

Often a starting point for her work, the materials themselves are chosen for their ability to communicate a particular story or sensibility. In recalling an overindulgent, imperial society on the brink of downfall, they bring to the fore questions of morality and acceptability. Each piece, then, is rooted in historical narrative, communicating silently a story of its own. Fascinated by the way in which our relationship with certain objects have shaped social history, Lingham's work speaks of a closeness between the wearer and the jewellery itself, allowing for a sense of personal intimacy and association.

1. *Black Tulips*
Adornment
Compressed cotton,
feathers, lace
26 x 102 cm
2005

2. *Pheasant Balls*
Necklace
Pheasant feathers, silver,
compressed cotton
35 cm drop
2005

1. *Multi-combs Hairpiece Necklace*
Silver plated chain, wood, acetate, shell
2005
Photography:
Gustavo Camillo

2. *Pearl Collar*
Silk, freshwater pearls
2005
Photography:
Gustavo Camillo

3. (overleaf)
Hood Necklace
Cotton, silver plated chain
2005
Photography: Gustavo Camillo

4. *Comb Glasses*
Eyewear/Hairpiece
Acetate, silver plated chain, glasses legs
2005
Photography: Gustavo Camillo

Husam El Odeh

Husam El Odeh's approach to jewellery making is as avant-garde as the jewellery he creates. "I start my work in quite an odd way", he explains. "I collect things I find, write snapshots of thoughts, cut things up, rearrange them and generally play with things that capture my interest." Constantly experimenting with materials and form, El Odeh's pieces take shape through an organic approach to making, becoming jewellery as they are constructed rather than being the product of fixed designs. El Odeh's dramatic work is a successful fusion of contradictory materials and objects that balance tactile and visual qualities, with iconically feminine pearls set against starched silk lapels in his *Pearl Collar* piece, or silver alongside shell and simple acetate hair accessories in *Hairpiece Necklace*. "I like setting opposites against each other", says El Odeh of his work. "I once made bangles out of tin and gold plated them; they felt incredibly cheap and expensive at the same time. I am always curious about materials, the way they feel, look, evoke and interact."

Continually gracing the pages of high-end fashion magazines and catwalk shows, El Odeh's background as a fine artist informs his conceptual yet wearable jewellery, citing art luminaries Meret Oppenheim and André Breton as key influences. "My jewellery is ideally surprising yet elegant", El Odeh notes. "Sometimes a bit hard but always full of contradiction and questions."

TIFFANY PARBS

Challenging and expanding contemporary definitions of jewellery, Tiffany Parbs' most recent designs are not for the faint-hearted. Inventive and conceptual, Parbs sees her ephemeral jewellery as "an ongoing investigation into the residue left by jewellery, the way the marks or sensations resonate on the skin long after the piece has been removed". Selecting a series of pertinent words including 'etch', 'itch', 'bruise', 'pucker', 'clamp', 'restrict' and 'burn', Parbs set out to create jewellery that would inflict diverse and transient effects on the wearer. Her *Skin Stamps* imprint the word 'etch' on the skin, while a temporary rash results from an application of the *Rash Stamps*. Bruises accompany the employment of the menacing knuckleduster *Abash* piece and the *Blister Ring* literally causes a sore bearing the word 'burn'.

Inspired by the groundbreaking abstract jewellers of the 1970s, Parbs is intrigued by "The items and articles that people allow into intimate space. I am especially intrigued by the features and embellishments the body absorbs over time." Through the harmless application of her *Marked* series of creations, Parbs demonstrates the way skin surfaces can be gently manipulated to respond to ephemeral embellishments and can transmute into temporary articles of jewellery.

1. *Abash Knuckledusters*
Silver, patina
9 x 1.2 x 3.8 cm
2005
Photography: Terence Bogue

2. Blister Ring
Skin
2005
Photography: Terence Bogue

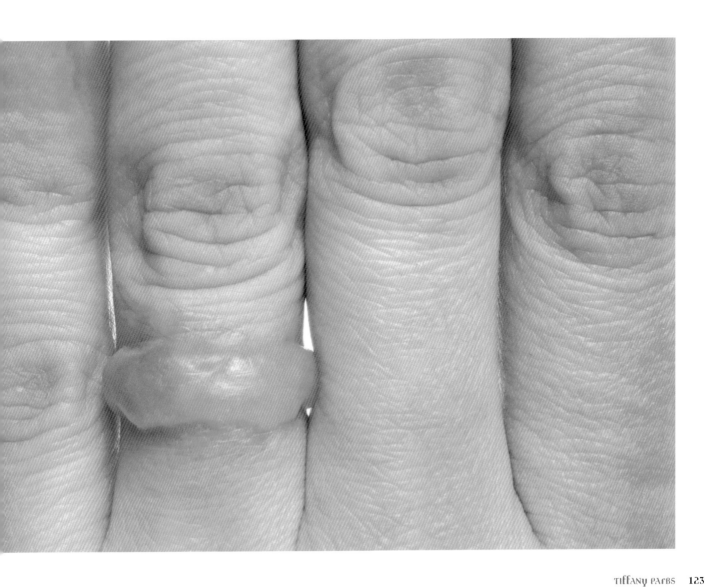

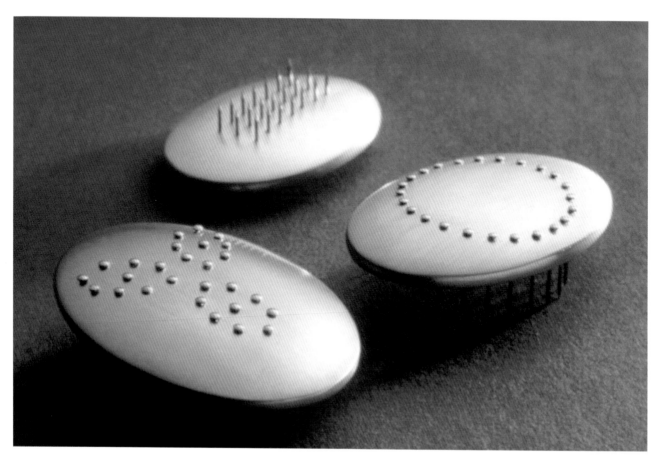

 3. *Rash Stamps*
Silver, nickel pins
2004
Photography: Greg Harris

4. *Rash Stamps*
Rash stamp application,
temporary rash
2004
Photography: Greg Harris

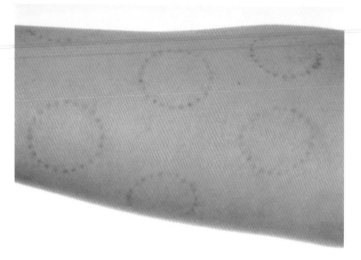

5. *Etched (pulse)*
Ephemeral bracelet
Skin
2004
Photography: Greg Harris

salima thakker

Evolving from processes of experimentation, trial and error, the designs of Salima Thakker are born from the unexpected, taking their forms from the unknown. The designer explains: "I never put my ideas down on paper, I proceed directly from the material, experimenting, making large numbers of samples, searching for forms, movements or surfaces that excite me. I am constantly looking for the unexpected beauty which can lay in the smallest of details."

Working in a range of extreme forms, she bends, cuts and folds each piece, experimenting with the boundaries of her chosen materials, pushing them to their limits, processing and redefining them to suit her individual visions. Pieces prioritise durability and longevity, in the belief that jewellery should be strong enough to endure centuries of wear and tear, that it should suit different trends and be applicable to different fashions and preferences. Made from gold, silver and other precious metals and stones – such as aquamarine and green tourmaline – each design is conceived to fit the wearer almost as a second skin, merging with their body to become one. Thakker's works are defined by exquisite and delicate craftsmanship; infused with movement and vitality – both literally, in the three-dimensional sense, and graphically, in the two-dimensional sense – they are always striking in their aesthetic and physical presence.

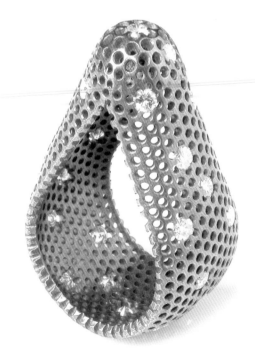

1. Ring
Silver, diamonds
2006

2. Ring
Silver, gold, green tourmaline
3.8 x 2.3 cm
2004

3. Bracelet
Patinated silver, gold
19 x 4.5 x 0.5 cm
2006

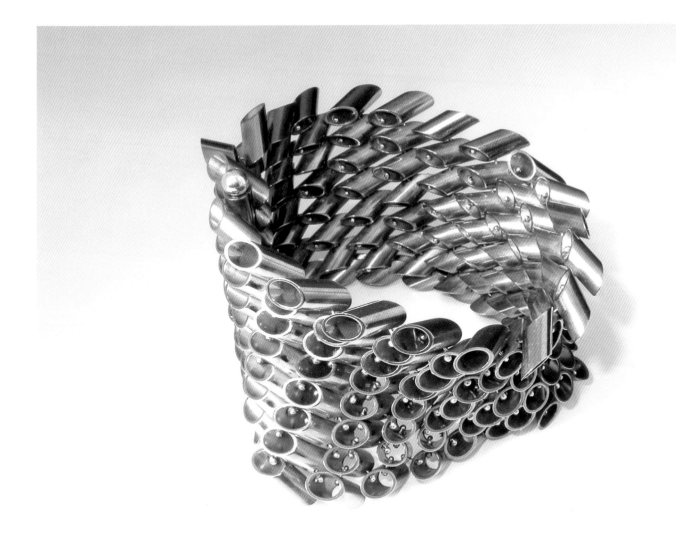

SMALL THINGS IN A WIDE WORLD

Roseanne Bartley

Machteld van Joolingen

Teresa Milheiro

Shari Pierce

Katja Prins

Francis Willemstijn

For your safety

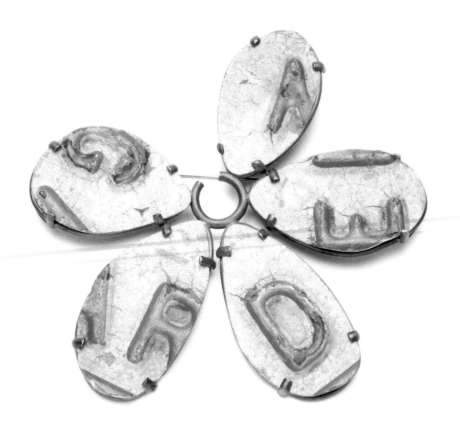

Roseanne Bartley

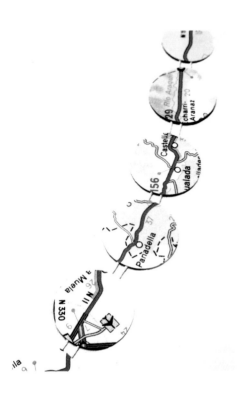

"When I find myself questioning the rationale of the world around me, my craft gives me the space to look upon something that is essentially rubbish and to contemplate making something else of it. The outcome may even be beautiful."

Inspired by the sense of liberation experienced when travelling overseas, Auckland-born designer Roseanne Bartley collects, hoards and transforms the detritus of her surroundings, bringing life and meaning to the myriad of discarded images that inspire her pieces. Through a process of 'surface archaeology', jewellery is formed from a variety of found materials and everyday items – from foreign train tickets to maps, safety instruction cards and car number plates – as well as the more conventional additions of silver, stainless steel and plastic. Whether personal or universal, each piece reveals something of a wider, more complex context. As a comment upon the Americanisation of society, *One on Every Corner*, for example, is a small crown-shaped brooch made predominantly from a plastic ring of McDonald's take-away spoons. The piece overtly references the worldwide permeation of society by fast food chains; while aesthetically pleasing and wearable, it also takes on a deeper, more critical agenda.

Bartley perceives jewellery as an ideal medium through which to view and communicate with the world. Her work is tinted consistently by the social, political and cultural, by personal experiences of different environments and situations and by the emotions that such experiences evoke. Intimate and fragile in nature, many are impermanent. The maker explains: "Using the simplest of tools and techniques, I make work with what is immediate. Made from ephemera, when worn, these pieces may only last the day, but like writing, drawing or photography, they are a way of grounding my experience of travel in a tangible form."

machteld van joolingen

"The attraction of jewellery is that it is so close to us. I have always liked and been inspired by the ritual, symbolism and story told when it is worn."

Tapping into the imagery and mystery of traditional folklore, Van Joolingen combines the past and present to create delicate-looking jewellery, infused with both personal and universal experience and imagery. Taking inspiration from different countries and cultures, he picks out patterns, textures, and symbols, transforming them into fresh forms, injecting them with new meaning and context. The designer explains: "One aspect of folklore is the visual integration of big changes within one society or another – changes which we do not yet understand and, therefore, [as artists] seek to conjure." Van Joolingen's work serves as a discrete and personal commentary upon the social and political occurrences that permeate contemporary cultures worldwide. Enchanted by the documentary photographs of daily newspapers and magazines, of Internet sites and television news, he employs the technique of photo etching, working with sheets of paper-thin metals so that pieces can be built up from many varied parts. Here, figures stride expressively from spiralling floral patterns; organic shapes engulf the faces of men, women and children, expressively rendered in a complex cut-out surfaces. Light and wearable, each one is imbued with narrative. Designs and patterns extracted from different cultural sources are etched individually, and combined into jewelleries that can be worn on the body in multiple ways – attached to a man's shirt, for example, or hung from lengths of black elastic designed to be hooked over each of the wearer's arms. Labelled by the maker as "Bodyplaques", they are envisaged as "flat statements of a changing world" – as intricate expressions of one man's view of a society that faces, unceasingly, great challenges and perpetual confrontation.

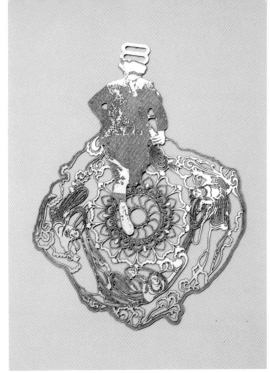

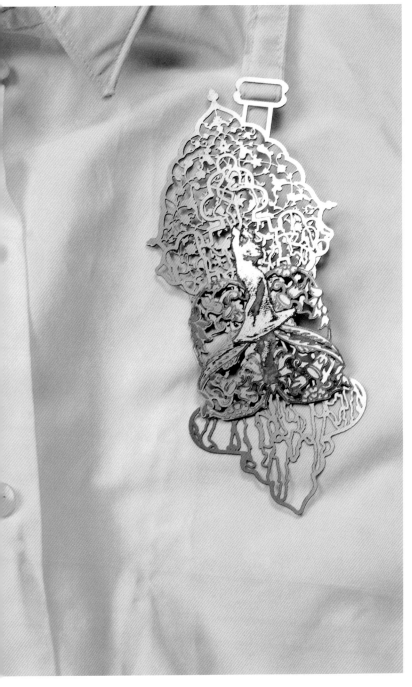

2. *Dancer Hanger*
Stainless steel
17 x 7.5 cm
2006
Photography: Rene van Wÿch

3. *Running Afghan Hanger*
Stainless steel
13 x 8.5 cm
2003
Photography: Rene van Wÿch

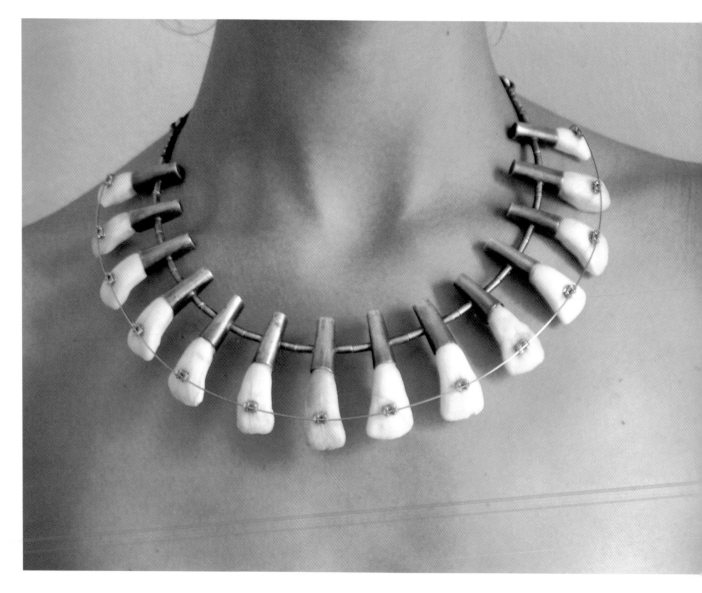

1. *The Aunt's Cow
Wears Braces*
Necklace
Oxidised silver, cows' teeth,
braces
21 x 19 cm
2004
Photography: Luis Pais

Teresa Milheiro

Through the development of an especially poignant and politically charged body of work, Teresa Milheiro directly challenges modern society's persistent obsessions with physical image. Focusing upon the increasingly unhealthy and widespread predilection for perpetual youth and beauty, she seeks to highlight, via an intense engagement with social precepts, the dangerous, unobtainable ideals that typically pervade contemporary cultures. Pointedly situating itself between the spheres of art, fashion, politics and science, her work, while enchanting and aesthetically striking, is irrefutably unconventional. Like miniature pieces of medical apparatus, pieces stand as intricate sculptures infused with meaning and upheld by context. While some adorn the body in the manner of traditional jewellery, around the neck or pinned to the breast, others are designed to fit between the lips, running from the mouth downwards: a clinical combination of plastic and metal. In a world where perfection is everything, Milheiro adopts a political, social and cultural stance, designing to challenge and confront and, sometimes, to shock and disturb. Cows' teeth, metal syringes, catheters, rubber tubing and bones are carefully combined in complex pieces that blend the natural and unnatural, with arresting consequences. Secured around the wearer's neck by a heavy ball and chain, a small portable botox kit designed to "kick out your wrinkles anywhere" draws attention to the pressure placed upon women to conform to unnatural aesthetic ideals. It hangs heavy from the body, cold and hard in appearance, basic in colour, reminiscent of a tiny torture instrument. Inspired by the detritus of the medical world, the tools of plastic surgeons and the equipment of those seeking to 'perfect' the human form, Milheiro combines unorthodox materials to form a collection rich in meaning, aggressive in form yet expertly crafted and surprisingly beautiful to behold.

2. *Be Botox*
Be Fucking Beautiful
Necklace
Oxidised silver, old syringe
2005
Photography: Luis Pais

3. *Survival Kit*
Object
Silver, catheters, rubber
mouth piece
2005
Photography: Luis Pais

4. *Be Botox*
Be Fucking Beautiful
Necklace
Oxidised silver, old syringe
2005
Photography: Luis Pais

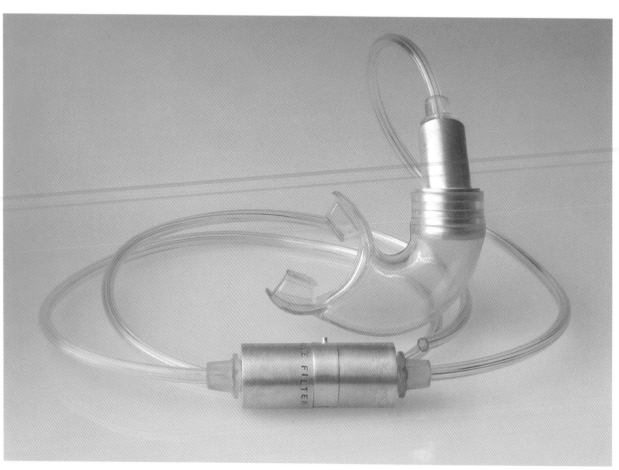

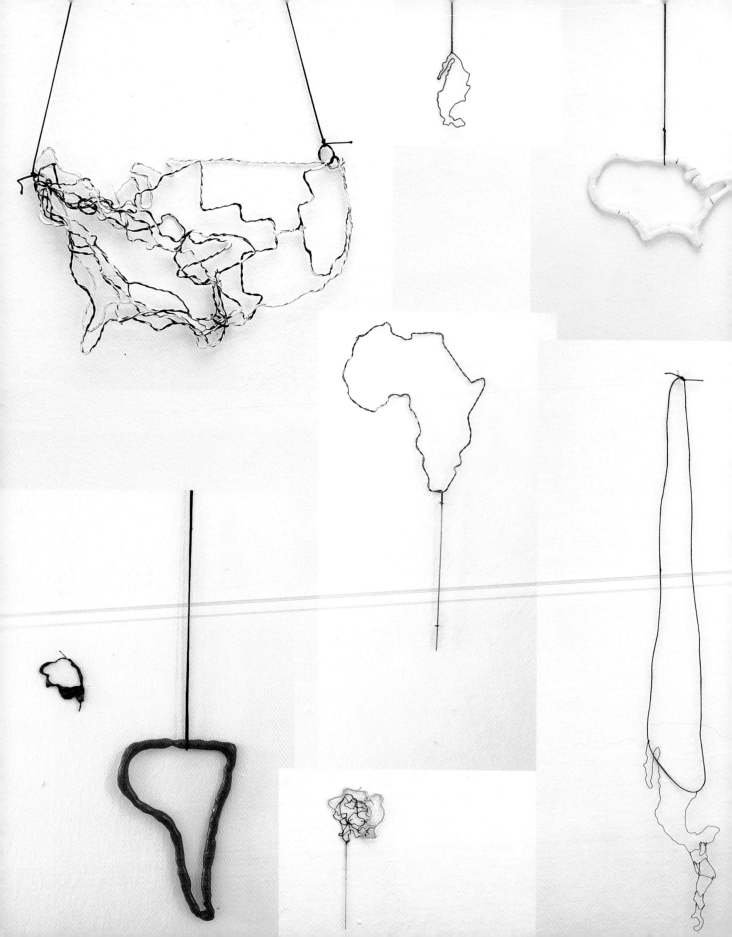

shari pierce

1. (clockwise from top left)
USA 1775–Present
Necklace
15.25 x 8.9 cm

Going North
Necklace
16.5 x 3.8 cm

USA
Pendant
14 x 7.6 cm

Mexico
Necklace
3 x 7.6 cm

Anonymous Border
Pendant
1.25 x 2.5 cm

South America
Pendant
6.3 x 10 cm

Anonymous Border
Pendant
1.25 x 2.5 cm

Africa
Pin
10 x 6.3 cm

Steel, industry enamel
2004

A piece of jewellery can be an expression of all kinds: a means for the wearer to declare themselves a member of a particular social class or group; to demonstrate wealth; to affirm an association with another person or a family; to proclaim difference or, indeed, sameness, by setting or following trends. Jewellery is rarely overtly associated with the political; it is more commonly perceived as a decoration or frivolity, a luxury, an addition to the necessity of clothing – something worn for its aesthetic value. We have long since disregarded the idea of jewellery as a fundamental means of displaying identity, but it is hard to find a culture that exists without any. And just as clothing is seen to be necessarily functional, in this society it is less and less so, and more of a luxury than ever. In a Western culture driven by consumption, the market and our wardrobes, drawers and dressing-tables are overflowing with possessions, far beyond our basic needs. And luxury goods are so readily available that we need never think beyond the transaction, over the counter or online, that adds one more superfluous thing to our hoard.

Yet any consumer item has a history of manufacture, from the sourcing of materials, through production, to distribution, which is shaped in part by socio-economic forces. Raw materials, whether hand-crafted and branded into a unique status symbol, or mass-manufactured into disposable high street goods, have a provenance which is at times questionable or exploitative; the market value of precious metals and stones is, in many parts of the world, rarely in proportion to the wages of those that mine and source them, and the damage to the environment is often, too, overlooked.

Shari Pierce's work addresses the history of exploitation and the present political climate in both material, execution and concept. The title of her series *Cardboard Democracy* refers to those politically unstable states that lay claim to a democracy which, in practice, is rife with corrupt and coercive measures. It is perhaps, too, a pointed reference to democracy in general as a constructed ideology, a seemingly universal good which the West upholds as a panacea to the world's problems, when in fact it might be argued that the buoyant economies upon which those very Western democracies are built are dependent upon the rich resources of far poorer states. This fragility is reflected in the materials she employs – cardboard, wire, paint – capable of holding a temporary shape but subject to wear and damage; offering a place of temporary refuge, but ultimately impermanent. In using cardboard, Pierce is perhaps also making reference to homelessness and the privations of street living, testifying to those who are disenfranchised by consumer societies. The majority of the material she uses is found or given – old cans of housepaint, fake metal chains from old costume jewellery – so that she is reusing what is cast aside and refashioning it into something of value.

2. Cardboard Democracy
Necklace
Cardboard box, interior &
exterior paint, metal chain
40.7 x 8.2 cm
2006

Starting with a cardboard box, sometimes "found while walking down the street… begging to be taken home", she plays upon the different ways that an empty vessel, ultimately made to be disposed of when its purpose is served, can signify. As Pierce notes, we see these boxes discarded in heaps at the supermarket; but equally, they can be "temporary houses for our most important memories and possessions", and, in the hands of a child, become a vehicle for imagination, with "limitless uses" – a fort, a castle, a car. In this way, then, this humble material is layered with meaning, in just the way that the material itself is constructed of layers of paper that can be "constructed and reconstructed multiple times".

Creating cut-outs and shaped wire outlines of countries, states, and continents, she examines the notion of defined borders and imposed divisions – between peoples, lands, languages, and cultures. Taken as a pure outline, the recognisable shapes of these pieces, stripped of their geo-political origin, reveal the often arbitrary nature of those divisions, and question the authority behind the mapping and claiming of territory. Malleable and delicate in appearance, they reveal the instability of defined boundaries; and in reducing the proportions of these vast spaces to something that can be held and crushed in the hand, she questions their very substance. These small statements then, seemingly flimsy in form, take on the vast and intangible concepts of territory, history, and politics. No longer purely luxury items, this jewellery becomes a means of expressing ideas in a manner more commonly associated with fine art practice. And it is all the more effective in doing so by being worn upon the body, pinned or hung in the very places that we ordinarily wear our self-indulgence.

3. *Cardboard Democracy*
Necklace
Cardboard box, interior &
exterior paint, metal chain
25.4 x 2.5 cm
2006

4. *Cardboard Democracy*
Bracelet
Cardboard box, interior &
exterior paint, metal chain
6.5 x 10 cm
2006

5. *Cardboard Democracy*
Necklace
Cardboard box, interior &
exterior paint, metal chain
39 x 4.5 cm
2006

1. Brooch
Silver, glass, sealing wax
7 cm
2005
Photography: Eddo Hartmann

katja prins

Like a collection of under-sized medical apparatus, the jewellery of Katja Prins inhabits a surreal world of unexpected forms, fusing aesthetically the natural and unnatural, the human and manmade. Tidy but physically complex, pieces play out surreal juxtapositions, contrasting materials in effective yet startling combinations and arrangements. Prins considers the machine as an extension of our bodies, addressing the intimate relationship between the delicacy of the human body and the imposing strength of the mechanical device, of technology, industry and machinery. Fed by social, political and cultural context – by the contemporary drive towards the manipulation of the human flesh, in what can only be classified as a vain attempt to 'perfect' one's born identity – she seeks to question, challenge and provoke, instilling within the function of jewellery new purpose and ideals. Works that waver between the borders of art, jewellery design and sculpture, ambiguous in appearance and compact in size, form a loaded vocabulary designed to speak of wider issues, reflecting contemporary malaise and dissatisfaction.

Executed in expressive combinations of silver, rubber, porcelain, plastic and glass, pieces are inspired by the physicality of everyday appliances, by medical instruments, factories, scientific and cosmetic procedures, futurism, and manipulated bodies torn apart by technology, and while particular works have clearly been designed to dress the body, others lean more toward sculpture. Her brooches speak silently of the modern tendency toward body 'enhancement' – red wax, for example, symbolising the pain, lost blood, and secrecy of cosmetic interventions, and silver tubing the patient's assaulted veins. Inspired by the industrial photographs of Bernd & Hiller Brecher, her *Machines Are Us* collection alerts the viewer to the vulnerability and fallibility of the human body. These small yet imposing *objets d'art*, with minimalist surface detail, are strong in concept, character and allusion; out of place and awkward as fashion accessories, they are always ambiguous.

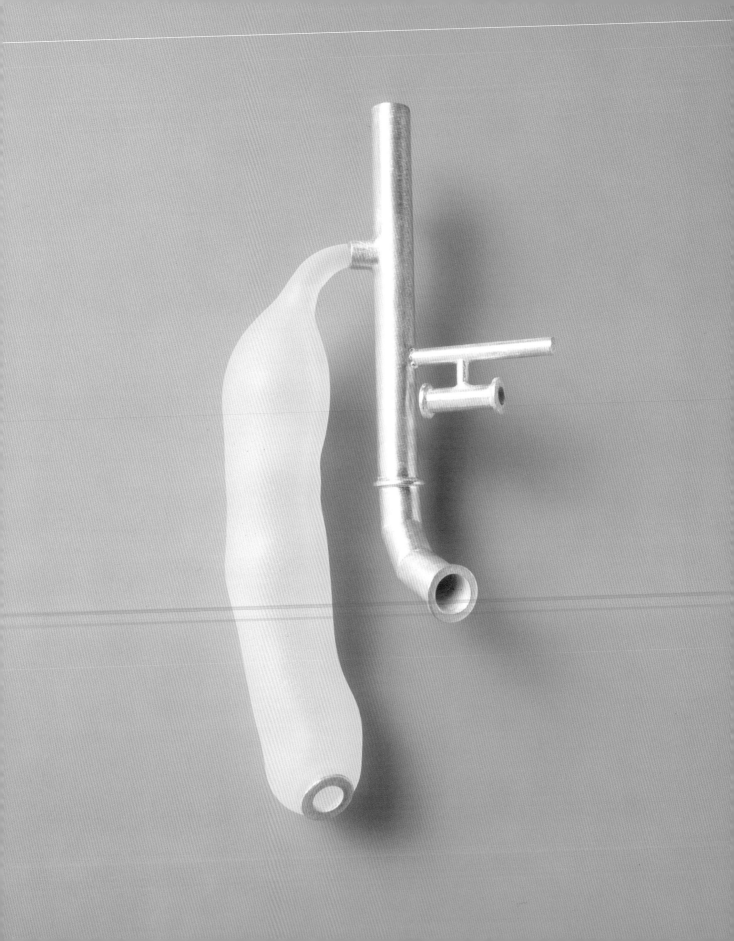

4. Brooch
Silver, plastic
9.5 cm
2005
Photography: Eddo Hartmann

2. Brooch
Silver, glass
8 cm
2005
Photography: Eddo Hartmann

3. Brooch
Silver, plastic
3.5 cm
2004
Photography: Eddo Hartmann

fRancis willemstijn

Francis Willemstijn delves into Dutch history with her haunting, beautifully crafted jewellery. Her works hark back to the seventeenth century, with authentic remains such as buttons and coins taking the place of jewels, and literal representations of sailing ships, coat of arms and family crests informing contours. "I feel connected to Dutch history", explains Willemstijn. "I try to translate my heritage, the clay of my own country into jewellery. My work is based on traces of the past which may soon disappear forever." Aspiring to create jewellery that conveys a story, Willemstijn employs materials that connect with the source of her inspiration – Dutch land and history. Ebony and rosewood, viewed as luxurious materials centuries ago, feature prominently in her works, Bog Oak (oakwood submerged in swamps for countless years) makes a frequent appearance as well as silver, gold and cotton. Willemstijn is creatively driven by the unique history of the materials she chooses to work with, saying, "These materials are very precious to me – their history and value mean more to me than diamonds."

To produce her evocative pieces, Willemstijn meticulously slices into thick silver plate, leaving the edges rough, emphasising the hand-made quality of her work. As a reaction against mass-production, Willemstijn creates pieces that cannot be reproduced, using unusual and often rare materials to produce elegant, avant-garde jewellery with an embedded memory and history. Willemstijn explains: "The pieces are a connection between past and present, tradition and innovation, life and death."

2. *Ground*
Necklace
Gold, silver, 17th century
coins, iron, wood
40 cm Ø
2004

3. *Grief*
Brooch
Gold, rosewood
6 cm
2004

CAMEOS AND KEEPSAKES

melanie bilenker

kim buck

lin cheung

cassandra chilton

julia deville

rory hooper

eija mustonen

julia turner

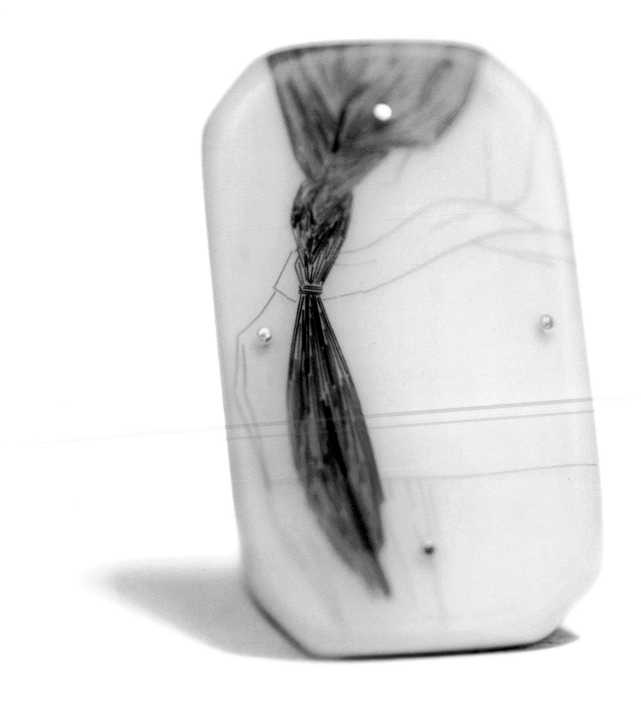

meLAnie biLenker

1 | **2**

1. *Braid*
Brooch
Silver, gold, ebony, resin,
pigment, hair
3.2 x 1.9 x 0.7 cm
2006
Photography: Ken Yanoviak

2. *A Day For a Bath*
Brooch
Gold, piano key ivory,
resin, hair
2.8 x 2.2 x 1.2 cm
2005
Photography: Kevin Sprague

Drawing upon historical notions of Victorian 'keepsakes' or sentimental objects, Melanie Bilenker creates intricate small-scale jewellery that functions as a reminder of eras, places and people. Constructing miniature line drawings using strands of hair, Bilenker painstakingly recreates portraits of loved ones or fleeting everyday moments, crafting objects that encapsulate memories. "I have always collected keepsakes and tokens, physical reminders of things. That is what I try to create, reminders of moments that I may forget – objects to capture them." Using the hair from the subject of her portraits, Bilenker references mourning jewellery and portrait miniatures of the 1800s, where hair was commonly used to create mementos for loved ones during times of unions or loss, marriage or death. While conceptually, Bilenker's work is closely related to this historical practice, its production and style is unique and contemporary. Using hair and other materials that have embedded memories, including antique piano keys and wood, alongside traditional gold and silver, Bilenker painstakingly arranges her designs using photographs as a guide then sets the work in resin. Each piece contains up to 2,000 strands of hair, with several layers creating the foreground and background of naturalistic, quiet domestic scenes. Far from mere ornaments, Bilenker's nostalgic jewellery offers a glimpse into moments passed, inviting close inspection.

3. *Dressing*
Brooch
Silver, gold, piano key ivory,
resin, hair
3.5 x 2.4 x 0.8 cm
2004
Photography: Kevin Sprague

4. *Drawing a Bath*
Brooch
Silver, gold, ebony, resin,
pigment, hair
5.4 x 4.4 x 0.9 cm
2006
Photography: Ken Yanoviak

5. *A Bath*
Brooch
Silver, gold, piano key ivory,
resin, hair
3.5 x 2.2 x 1 cm
2004
Photography: Kevin Sprague

6. *The Top Shelf*
Brooch
Silver, gold, piano key ivory,
resin, hair
2.2 x 2.8 x 0.8 cm
2004
Photography: Kevin Sprague

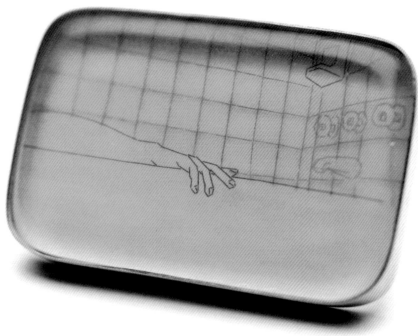

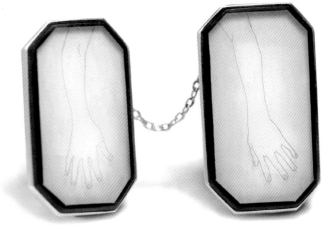

7. *Arms*
Brooch
Silver, gold, piano key ivory,
resin, hair
2 x 3.4 x 0.7 cm each
2005
Photography: Ken Yanoviak

kim buck

"My jewellery is about jewellery", award-winning goldsmith Kim Buck explains laconically of his elegant, skilfully crafted designs – though simple, it is an apt statement. Buck's delicate pieces reflect on the fundamental basis of jewellery – wearability and communicability. Buck creates jewellery that is to be worn, that will take on a new life once it leaves the hands of the maker: "The important thing about jewellery is what goes on after the pieces leave the maker, what they mean to people. Through my pieces I try to show my respect for this, and to visualise the aspects and values of jewellery that we as makers have no influence on, and can take no part in."

Utilising materials including gold, silver, pearls, diamonds and even metalled plastic foil on occasion, as in the *Gold Heart* inflatable brooch, Buck crafts and hand-finishes intricate rings, necklaces, pendants, brooches and objects using traditional and modern techniques. Using CAD/CAM (Computer Aided Designed and Computer Aided Manufacturing) software, Buck also employs conventional techniques, honed through his training as a goldsmith; as he says, "My education as a goldsmith is the basis for everything that I do. I am in a very traditional trade that I both respect and dislike – my recent work reflects these contrasting feelings and mechanisms."

1. *Gold Heart*
Inflatable brooch
Plastic foil
9.5 x 9.5 x 5.3 cm
2003
Photography: Dorte Krogh

2. *Faith, Hope and Charity*
Charm
750 gold and CIBA tool
7.3 x 7.3 cm
2005
Photography:
Anders Sune Berg

3. *Gold Heart*
Necklace
750 gold
1.2 cm
2001
Photography: Ole Akhøj

4. *Solitaire Ring*
750 gold
2001
Photography: Ole Akhøj

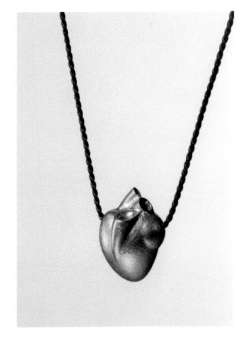

Lin Cheung

1. *Through and Through*
Necklace
Silver, gold
2005

2. *Golden Years*
Necklace
Silver, gold, silk
6 x 4 x 0.9 cm
2005

"I discovered that the reasons people gave for wearing jewellery intrigued me more than the actual items", Lin Cheung has explained of the driving force behind her work. Always informed by the wearer, and the ways in which what is worn becomes imbued with meaning, Cheung's *oeuvre* as a whole represents a fascinating, ongoing examination of the functions that jewellery serves and what is invested in it. Delving freely into historical jewelleries, she is part of a generation of contemporary makers that is referring back to traditional values and concepts, integrating them into her own unique, new forms. In contrast to the abstract minimalism of jewellers in the 1980s, which deliberately rejected this kind of continuity, she has taken this as a starting point, as part of her ongoing "analysis of the fundamental reasons for wearing jewellery". Exploring the symbolic and social functions that it serves, she takes on the forms and concepts of the past while retaining a very modern sensibility and aesthetic.

While there are pieces to inherit, there is also new jewellery to be acquired, which will come to fulfil a new symbolic function. Cheung asks: "When deliberately searching for a piece of jewellery that might embody sentiment, how do you know when you have found *the one*? ... Should it already be 'full' with another sentiment, partially full or empty?" A wedding or engagement ring, for example, has a pre-designated symbolic value that exists prior to the object itself. But the choice of the object that will carry that weight is of the utmost importance to the wearer; the ring must be worthy of the statement it embodies. There is a sense that the hole at the centre has been waiting to be filled by one particular finger. In contrast to an heirloom, in which meaning and jewel are commensurate, passed to new wearers who add to that heritage, the ring is a void until chosen by its wearer. As Cheung explains, "An interesting and perplexing aspect of jewellery to me is that a piece can at once mean everything to someone and nothing to another."

By heart, 2005, takes this idea as its starting point: the piece "examines the notion that a piece can just 'feel' right. Five identical looking pendants are distinguished apart only by touch." The pendants themselves have a clean, delicate aesthetic, recalling traditional lockets in their shape and in the use of silver, brushed to a soft sheen. A number of her pieces incorporate this basic locket form, addressing the idea that "To secure a definite, unwavering meaning a piece must be 'locked', completely sealed."

Cheung's 'locked lockets' are an attempt to "visualise the sentimental value of a piece of jewellery and the personal meanings placed onto it by the wearer that a viewer has no access to"; so the locket does not open, but has its meaning encrypted on the surface. *Breath/e* is one such piece; using a delicately engraved fragment of poetry by Paul Éluard, this sensuous work addresses the very concept of intimacy. The way that the pendant functions – the words become more vivid when breathed upon – is founded upon a typically concise conceptual framework. It is inspired by the technique of the antique expert, breathing upon silver to find the seams in an antique piece, in order to determine value and age; but as the 'viewer' would need to draw close to the neck of the wearer to read the words, the *Breath/e* of the title is also that of Éluard's "Lover".

Hidden value, 2006, is a necklace made entirely of lockets, 'mounted' like precious stones; it gives away no secrets. As Cheung observes, "Whether a locket is full or empty, the perception of preciousness is in the concept of the locket itself: believing that it should contain something of value." So, again, this work takes a recognisable form and plays upon shared perceptions to convey its meaning.

While Cheung's work is highly conceptual in nature, it is also highly wearable; indeed, desirability and accessibility are very much knit up in her conceptual framework. The purity of her form is the result of a desire to keep the jewellery free of extraneous, "unnecessary decoration… that would detract from the overall meaning of what I wanted to say with a particular piece… using recognisable jewellery forms eases the way an idea can be communicated."

3. *Breath/e*
Pendant
Silver, text from "Lover"
by Paul Éluard
2005

4. *Hidden Value*
Necklace
Gold
2006

Moira

Lyndal

Julia

Cassandra

CΛSSΛNDRA CHILTON

Known for her 'Victorian Pop' brand of jewellery design, Cassandra Chilton is unconventional in many respects – notably that she is a practising landscape architect. Perhaps inspired by this, and the environmental artists of the 1960s who saw landscape as a site for art, Chilton views the human body as a site for her jewellery – aiming to "enhance the visibility and individuality of the wearer".

Drawing upon the typology of the cameo brooch, Chilton reworks this traditional archetype, placing it in a modern context. Where cameos were historically the product of hand carving or moulding of a relief image, Chilton uses modern technology to incise two-dimensional shapes out of coloured acrylic sheets. The technique and materials are contemporary, but the subject matter draws upon historic references such as seventeenth and eighteenth century European brooches and Victorian silhouette portraits. Her *Collingwood Ladies* series of brooches sandwiches together delicate silhouette portraits upon vibrant and elaborately decorative, mechanically cut, background surfaces or 'frames'. The *from a distance looks like flies* brooches continue this theme but deviate from the usual subject matter of a woman's profile to the unexpected visage of an insect – elevated to the status of art object. The insect pieces are inspired by entomology collection boxes, where the decorative specimen brooches, says Chilton, "parallel the intricacy of the insects' silhouettes with the baroque lines of the cameo setting".

1 2

1. *Drawn with a Very Fine
Camelhair Brush*
Portraits
2005

2. *The Collingwood Ladies*
Brooches
Acrylic, 925 silver,
stainless steel
2005

Specimens
(Coleoptera)

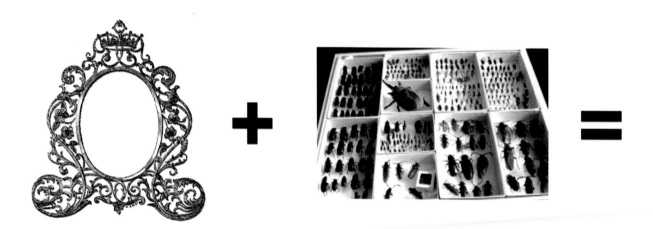

3 **4**

3. *from a distance
looks like flies*
Concept drawings
2005

4. (clockwise from
top left)
Staghorn (Lucanida)

*Scarab
(Scarabaeidae)*

*Longhorn
(Cerambycidae)*

Brooches
Acrylic, 925 silver,
stainless steel
10 x 12.5 cm
2005

1. *Bird-Pin*
Bird, natural diamonds,
9ct & 18ct gold
16.5 x 2.5 x 1.5 cm
2004
Photography: Terence Bogue

2. *Prey*
Brooch
Sterling silver, mouse, natural
topaz
2004
Photography: Greg Harris

JuliA Deville

At once exquisite and arresting, Julia DeVille's avant-garde designs, while referencing explicitly the history and traditions of jewellery, question predetermined notions of mortality and the Western perception of death as taboo. Inspired overtly by Victorian mourning jewellery and the memento mori of earlier centuries, DeVille, a trained taxidermist, casts organic matter in gold and sterling silver, transforming tiny lives into delicate pieces of wearable jewellery. Designing to provoke, she utilises a combination of alternative materials ranging from animal fur, feathers, hair and bone to the incorporation of small creatures, stuffed and mounted on glossy jet shields like a collection of exquisite hunting trophies. Juxtaposing these with luxury jewels, black pearl, ivory and coral, she demonstrates both an understanding of the traditional relationship between adornment and death, and an informed engagement with the contemporary treatment of animals within the spheres of leisure, art and fashion. Identifying with themes and issues that are often ignored, her work – employing only animals that have died of natural causes – seeks to celebrate death; which in turn, she believes, should be seen as a celebration of life. Each piece provokes a reevaluation of modern standards, questioning our current obsessions with life extension and preservation. "I use the symbols of death throughout my work", explains DeVille, "because I think it is important to identify with the concept that we are in fact mortal creatures. The nature of our culture is to obsess over planning the future, however in doing so, we often forget to enjoy the present." As other, non-Western cultures perceive death as a positive occurrence, DeVille inspires both a respect for life and a constructive contemplation of its end, successfully challenging preconceived notions of beauty, fear, and morality.

3. *Gunclub*
Brooch
Mouse, natural diamonds, jet,
9ct & 18ct gold
2004
Photography: Greg Harris

4

4. *Mouse-Pin*
Mouse, natural rubies,
sterling silver, 18ct gold
16.5 x 2.5 x 1.5 cm
2004
Photography: Terence Bogue

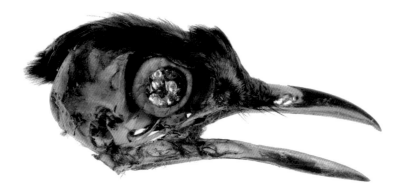

5. *Jet Mourning Brooch*
Jet, 9ct gold
4 x 2 x 1 cm
2004
Photography: Terence Bogue

6. *Bird Skull*
Brooch
Bird skull, cubic zirconia,
sterling silver
5 x 2.5 x 3 cm
2004
Photography: Greg Harris

Rory Hooper

Distinctive and thought provoking, Rory Hooper explores a multiplicity of poignant themes through his jewellery-making and design process. From subjects as diverse as Jewish history to mass-production, Hooper reflects his myriad concerns through a preoccupation with abandoned material. Abstracting and reinventing discarded items of jewellery, Hooper not only reinvests the objects with meaning and worth, but also questions the disposable nature of contemporary consumer society. Hooper's most recent series features a vast array of used jewellery including rings, earrings, bracelets and necklaces. He explains: "The name of this project was chosen through an interpretation of the term 'chewing gum', as a symbol of cultural leftover. Chewing gum is a common product symbolising lack of manners and depth – it sticks everywhere but is then forgotten."

Hooper, with one blow of a hammer, flattens the abandoned jewellery he reinvents – each object receiving identical treatment as though by machine. Crushing the gold jewellery in this fashion is a metaphor for industrial labour and mass-production, but also inevitably brings about associations with Jewish 'beaten gold'. Once the jewellery has been flattened, often the pieces will be set with diamonds and other precious stones, which allows the jewellery, Hooper says, greater artistic and economic value. "The immediate association is an image of confiscated Jewish gold heaped in a great pile by the Nazis during World War II", explains Hooper of his pummelled pieces; "The Jewish gold and culture smashed by the Nazi hammer in systematic order through industrial violence."

1. *Chewing Gum*
234 pieces
Gold plated silver
2005
Photography:
Leonid Padrul Kwitkowski

2. *Bracelet 2*
Gold plated silver
10 cm
2005

3. *Chain of Chains 2*
Neckpiece
Silver
4 x 3 cm
2005

4. *Neckpiece 2*
Silver, string
12 x 12 cm
2006

5. *Chewing Gum*
Gold plated silver
2.5 x 4.5 cm
2005

6. *Chewing Gum*
Gold plated silver
2.5 x 3 cm
2005

1. *Ruttu*
Brooch
Leather, silver
7 x 12 cm
2006
Photography: Kimmo Heikkilá

2. *Mätäs*
Brooch
Leather, silver, resin
11 x 11 cm
2006
Photography: Kimmo Heikkilá

eiJa mustonen

Eija Mustonen has been using jewellery and sculpture as a means of artistic expression for nearly 20 years, viewing jewellery as "a communicator between human beings and the environment". Interested in the intimate relationship between jewellery and the body as well as the body's connection to its surroundings, the progressive Mustonen says, "Jewellery is valuable, and for me the most valuable thing is the landscape and space around me." Her interest in the built and natural environment is evident in her pieces, with a variety of natural materials such as leather, silver and thread fashioned together into organic shapes and forms. The *Mätäs* series of brooches embody this concept, each piece appearing animate, as though growing and expanding.

The jewellery-making process begins through the establishment of a principal theme, which then determines the materials to be employed. Despite several staple materials appearing throughout her work, part of Mustonen's artistic process is the notion of experimentation between material and form, which leads her to continually employ new and diverse materials appropriate to each design. The use of space as a concept for Mustonen transcends physical space to incorporate the "psychic state"; she explains: "The connection to my own environment is a starting point in my working process; randomness and order as it is in nature. The forms, colours and materials express my relationship to the space."

3. *Cameo Brooch*
Cameos, resin, silver
9 cm
2005
Photography: Kimmo Heikkilá

1. *Estelle Brooch*
Maple, 18ct gold, glass head
pins, stain
5 x 5 x 1 cm
2006

2. *Black Prong Brooch*
Ebony, 18ct gold
6 x 6 x 1 cm
2005

3. *Black Lines Brooch*
Ebony, gesso, sterling silver
6.5 x 6.5 x 1 cm
2001
Photography: George Post

Julia Turner

For Julia Turner, the creation of jewellery is analogous to the attempt to express oneself in words, particularly in the words of an unfamiliar or foreign language. As each language has countless expressions and nuances, so too does each jewellery design. "When I make jewellery", the designer explains, "I feel that I am mining a language, looking at its early beginnings and current usage all with the same eye, and that my job isn't so much to invent meaning as to simply notice where it's been sitting all along, waiting for somebody to dig it out." Turner returns repeatedly to jewellery's own history and traditions, extracting a variety of forms and archetypes to be employed in the creation of something new and unique. Using such references as a platform for the development of her work, Turner seeks to engage and explore the power that jewellery has to "contain or represent memory, experience, desire and sorrow" – all constituting a particular kind of wealth when gathered together or displayed upon the same body. Taking inspiration from the daily observations of herself and others, she builds her own visual language, rooted in reality and consistent in terms of artistic technique and expressive form. Jewelleries are formed from the desire to push a certain material or process to its breaking point; to resolve inherent tensions between materials, lines, surfaces and space. The designer explains: "As I experiment more and more with a specific approach and become more discerning about what I see emerging, I begin to see the unnecessary elements fall away and the 'real' piece of jewellery emerge. Though I set formats and limits for the sake of continuity, I often find myself applying the same technique to multiple materials just to see how they will respond."

Made from a combination of gold and silver as well as lighter, softer materials such as maple, linen, ebony, glass and gesso, her pieces are visually striking, executed in a range of vivid blues and reds; imposing monotones are juxtaposed with textured surfaces, flecked with delicate patterns and fine, wavering lines.

NATURAL SELECTION

kirsten bak

Born 1977, Aalborg, Denmark, where she currently lives and works.
Kirsten Bak initially undertook practical goldsmith studies at
Engelsholm Kunsthojskole, Danish Folk High School for Art in 1998,
followed by an exchange semester in 2002 at The University of Fine Art
in Braunschweig, completing a Bachelor of Fine Art Degree through
The University of Applied Sciences, Idar-Oberstein, Germany in 2005.
The same year she launched the eponymous BAKS agency for
contemporary jewellery and design. Bak's awards include the Innovation
Prize 2006, *Inghorgenta*, Munich, and the 2001 DAAD for foreign
students at The University of Applied Sciences, Trier, Germany.

Selected exhibitions
2006 *SOFA*, New York, represented by Charon Kransen Arts
2006 *Skandal*, 15th International Silver Art Competition, State Art
Gallery of Legnica, Poland

Selected publications
Metalsmith, Spring 2006

ela bauer

Born 1960, Warsaw, lives and works in Amsterdam.
Having initially studied Comparative Literature and Indology at The
Hebrew University in Jerusalem, 1982–1987, Ela Bauer went on to study
Jewellery at the Technical School in Jerusalem for a year, before moving
on to the Gerrit Rietveld Academy in Amsterdam in 1990 to continue
her studies, graduating in 1995. Her work is held in a number of galleries'
and private collections, including the Grassi Museum in Leipzig, and
the Hiko Mizuno Collection in Tokyo. Over her ten-year career she
has shown work in Lisbon, Detroit, San Francisco, Paris, Tokyo, and
numerous other cities. She has been awarded grants from the Scholings
Foundation for Art and Culture and the Prins Bernhard Foundation,
both in The Netherlands, and stipends from the Foundation of Fine Arts
and Design, The Netherlands, in 2002 and 2005.

Selected exhibitions
2005 *Proximity, the Sensory and Displacement*, Wayne State University,
Detroit
2005 *Inspired by Nature?*, Gallery Platina, Stockholm
2004 *Recycling*, Annick Zufferey, Geneva

julie blyfield

Born 1957, Melbourne, lives and works in Adelaide.
Since 1987, Julie Blyfield has been a full-time partner in the Gray Street
Workshop in Adelaide. In 1987–1988, she studied Jewellery Making
and Silversmithing at the South Australian College of the Arts and
Education, having completed a Diploma in Teaching ten years previously.
Alongside her jewellery work, which is widely exhibited and held in
collections from Australia to Scotland and the Czech Republic, she has
also worked on architectural commissions, designing interiors, signage,
monuments, and various decorative elements. In 2002–2003, a grant
from Arts South Australia allowed her to undertake a Residency with
Frank Bauer and develop a solo exhibition. She was awarded a New Work
Established Grant by the Visual Arts/Craft Board of Australia in 2004.

Selected exhibitions
2006 *Transformations: The Language of Craft*, National Gallery of
Australia, Canberra
2005 *Signs Taken for Wonders*, Galerie Ra, Amsterdam, and University
Gallery, South Australia
2004 *SOFA*, New York, represented by Charon Kransen Arts

sebastian buescher

Born 1978, Cologne, lives and works in Brighton, UK
Sebastian Buescher has trained in a number of disciplines over the
course of his career; having graduated from a Bachelor of Arts in
Graphic Information Design from the University of Westminster,
London, in 1998, he has gone on to take a further Bachelor's degree in
Silversmithing, Jewellery and Allied Crafts from London Metropolitan
University in 2003, and has taken courses in Ceramics and Glassblowing.
Having worked as an artist's assistant in London in 2005, he is currently
lecturing at the Surrey Institute of Art and Design in the UK. In 2003,
he was awarded The Worshipful Company of Goldsmiths' First Prize; his
work is held at the Alice and Louis Koch Collection in Switzerland.

Selected exhibitions
2006 *SOFA*, New York, represented by Charon Kransen
2006 *Koru 2*, South Karelia Art Museum, Lappeenranta, Finland
2005 *Christmas Exhibition*, Alternatives Gallery, Rome

karl fritsch

Born 1963, Sonthofen, Germany, lives and works in Munich.
Karl Fritsch undertook studies in jewellery at Goldsmiths' school in
Pforzheim until 1985, and was later educated at the Academy of Fine
Arts, Munich; he set up his workshop upon graduating in 1994. Fritsch
exhibits throughout the world and has work in numerous collections
including the Stedelijk Museum Amsterdam, Netherlands, The Helen
Drutt Collection, Philadelphia, and the Royal College of Art, London.
Fritsch guest lectures frequently at prestigious institutions such as the
Royal Melbourne Institute of Technology, Australia; Massachusetts
College of Art, Boston; Hiko Mizuno College of Jewellery, Tokyo; and
Bezalel University, Jerusalem. Awards include the international Françoise
van den Bosch Prize for contemporary jewellery in 2006.

Selected exhibitions
2005 Solo exhibition, Gallery Deux Poissons, Tokyo
2005 Solo exhibition, Gallery Sophie Lachaert, Tielrode, Belgium

Selected Publications
2004 *1000 Rings*, Asheville, NC: Lark Books, 2004

constanze schreiber

Born 1977, Siegen, Germany, lives and works in Amsterdam.
Since graduating with a Bachelor of Design in Jewellery from the
Gerrit Rietveld Academie, Amsterdam, in 2004, Constanze Schreiber
has undertaken Masterclasses with Kjell Nordstrom, and on 'Burned
Jewellery' with Otto Künzli. She has also given workshops and lectures
at Transarte in Utrecht, and at the Schmucksymposium Zimmerhof in
Germany in 2005 amongst others. Her work is held at the Marzee
Collection in Nijmegen, The Netherlands, and has been shown in various
galleries across Europe and more recently the USA. In 2005 she was
awarded a Dutch Design Prize.

Selected exhibitions
2007 *Collect*, London
2006 *Two Close Ones*, Estonian Museum of Applied Art and Design, Tallinn
2006 *Schmuck 2006*, Handwerksmesse, Munich and Museum of Art and Design, New York

PLAYTHINGS AND PARODIES

maisie broadhead

Born 1980, London, where she currently lives and works.
Since graduating from the Wood, Metal, Plastics and Ceramics BA at Brighton University in 2002, Maisie Broadhead has continued to produce jewellery for retail and private commissions and sold work in London and New York. She also continues to produce works for gallery exhibition. She is currently based at a jewellery studio in east London.

Selected Exhibitions
2006 *Artists Unknown*, The Black and White house gallery, London
2004 *Body Extensions*, MUDAC Museum of Design, Lausanne, Switzerland

sigurd bronger

Born 1957, Oslo, where he currently lives and works.
Bronger completed his degree at the MTS Vakschool, Schoonhoven in The Netherlands in 1979, and has since pursued a successful career as a jeweller. He has received a number of prizes and grants, including the Norwegian Design Award in 1997, and an Oslo City Culture Grant. His work is held in several public collections around Scandinavia and at the Stedelijk Museum in Amsterdam, and the Royal College of Art, London, and he has lectured and spoken at institutions and conferences in the UK, The Netherlands, and Germany.

Selected exhibitions
2002 *Lepels/Spoons*, Galerie Ra, Amsterdam
2001 Solo exhibition, Bergen Kunstforening, Bergen, Germany
2000 *The Decorated Ego*, Fabiola Zaal, Antwerp

arthur hash

Born 1976, Balboa, Panama, lives and works in Richmond, Virginia.
Arthur Hash has undertaken numerous teaching and instructors' positions, both at the institutions at which he has studied and elsewhere, alongside his own education at Virginia Commonwealth University, 1995–2001, and Indiana University, 2002–2005. The range of disciplines in which he has taught, including metalsmithing, 'Experimental Materials and Assemblage', enameling (in Rostov, Russia), 'Basic Milling and Lathe Operation', painting and printmaking, and sculpture, reflects the diversity of his own eclectic practice. Over the last eight years he has exhibited in numerous venues across the USA and elsewhere.

Selected exhibitions
2006 *Arthur Hash: Instance*, Quirk Gallery, Richmond, Virginia
2005 *Virtual/Tangible*, Reinberger Galleries, The Cleveland Institute of Art, Cleveland, Ohio

craig isaac

Born 1972, Winchester, UK, lives and works in London.
Craig Isaac began his studies at the Winchester School of Art in 1991, undertaking Foundation Studies in Art, followed by a Higher National Diploma in 1994 through the Epsom School of Art, and a Bachelor Degree with First Class Honours at Middlesex University in 1998. Currently Isaac is a Jewellery/Metals Senior Technician and Summer School Tutor at Middlesex University; in 1997 he was a gold, metals and silver technician at The Royal College of Art, London. His innovative designs have been featured in the leading UK publications *Dazed & Confused*, *Elle* and *The Big Issue*.

Selected exhibitions
1998 *Branching Out*, Gallery V&V, Vienna
1998 *Showing Off*, Institute of Contemporary Arts, London

felieke van der leest

Born 1968, Emmen, The Netherlands, lives and works in Amsterdam.
Felieke van der Leest graduated from the Gerrit Rietveld Academy in Amsterdam in 1996. In the ten years following, her jewellery has been exhibited in both group and solo exhibitions in Europe, the USA and Japan, and featured in numerous publications. The Museum of Decorative Arts in Montreal, the Museum of Modern Art in Arnhem, The Netherlands, the Royal Museum of Scotland in Edinburgh, and the Hiko Mizuno Collection in Tokyo are just some of the many collections, both private and public, that have purchased her unique work.

Selected exhibitions
2006 *Animal Fables*, solo exhibition, Middlesbrough Institute of Modern Art, Dorman Museum, Middlesbrough, UK
2005 *Ostriches in Love: the Wonderful Jewellery of Felieke van der Leest*, Dutch Textile Museum, Tilburg, The Netherlands
2005 *Proximity, the Sensory and Displacement*, Wayne State University, Detroit, USA

Selected publications
500 Brooches, Asheville, NC: Lark Books, 2005
Jucca, Spring/Summer 2004, Japan

lindsey mann

Born 1979, Winchester, UK, where she currently lives and works.
Lindsey Mann graduated from Middlesex University in 2002 with a Bachelor of Arts in Jewellery, after which she founded her jewellery practice and workshop with the aid of a Setting Up Grant from Arts Council South East London in 2003. In 2005, Mann won a Crafts Council Development Award, having obtained an Arts Council Grant through the prestigious Chelsea Crafts Fair a year earlier. Mann continues to work on educational projects with schools, colleges and galleries, as well as running workshops and evening classes from her studio.

Selected exhibitions
2006 *Art in Action*, Water Perry, Oxfordshire, UK
2005 *Style-O-Rama*, Leicester City Gallery, Leicester, UK
2005 *Bright Young Things*, Royal Birmingham Society of Arts, Birmingham, UK

marc monzó

Born 1973, Barcelona, where he currently lives and works.
Marc Monzó completed a Bachelor of Fine Art Degree at Escola Massana Centre of Art and Design in Jewellery, Engraving and Sculpture in 1996. In 1999–2000, Monzó undertook further study in stone paving. His intricate designs have been exhibited continuously throughout Europe in both solo and group exhibitions over the last ten years, with work appearing in the permanent collections of The Stedelijk Museum, The Netherlands as well as the Françoise van den Bosch Foundation, The Netherlands.

Selected exhibitions
2006 *Global Edit* by *Wallpaper** magazine, Armani Teatro, Salone di Mobile, Milan
2006 *Schmuck 2006*, Museum of Decorative Arts, New York
2006 *SOFA*, Gallery Ornamentum, New York

NOA Nadir

Born 1970, Israel, lives and works in Tel-Aviv.
Noa Nadir, a jewellery maker with a background in pottery, completed a Bachelor of Fine Art Degree in 1996 in Jewellery and Goldsmithing at Bezalel Academy of Art, Jerusalem, before undertaking a postgraduate degree at the same institution, graduating in 1997. Nadir, who runs an independent workshop for the crafting and design of jewellery, catering to private clientele, has been the recipient of various awards, including the Meizler Prize through the Bezalel school, and has exhibited work throughout Israel, as well as in Chicago, and Turnov in the Czech Republic.

Selected exhibititons
2005 *Beaten Gold: Israeli Jewellery 3*, Eretz Israel Museum, Tel-Aviv
2004 *SOFA*, Chicago

ted noten

Born 1956, Tegelen, The Netherlands, lives and works in Amsterdam.
Renowned maker and artist Ted Noten has enjoyed a prolific and successful career since studying at the Academy of Applied Arts in Maastricht, 1983–1986, and the Gerrit Rietveld Academie in Amsterdam, 1986–1990. Alongside his work as a jeweller, he has designed products, interiors and exhibitions, and is also a photographer and video artist. He is a respected lecturer who has taught at institutions as diverse as the Hiko Mizuno Jewellery College in Japan, the Design Academy, Eindhoven, and the Royal College of Art, London. The recipient of numerous grants and awards, his work is held in public collections including the Stedelijk Museum, Amsterdam, and the Musée des Arts Decorative, Montreal.

Selected exhibitions
2006 Solo exhibition, Gallery Deux Poissons, Tokyo
2006 *Tall Stories: Narrative Jewellery from The Netherlands*, Stedelijk Museum, Amsterdam
2005 *Blue*, Mobilia Gallery, Cambridge, MA, USA

Selected publications
Staal, Gert, *Ted Noten*, Rotterdam: Uitgeverij 010, 2005 Artworks and Objects

ARTWORKS AND OBJECTS

an alleweireldt

Born 1974, Ostend, Belgium, lives and works in London.
An Alleweireldt completed a Bachelor of Arts Product Design degree at Hogeschool, Antwerp in 1997, later undertaking a Master of Goldsmithing, Silversmithing, Metalwork and Jewellery at the Royal College of Art in London from 2000–2002. Currently Alleweireldt designs and creates jewellery through her company Oxx, through which she frequently takes on freelance jewellery design and production work for private clients and contemporary luxury brands. Alleweireldt has a number of project sponsors including Swarovski, and has her work available to purchase in numerous boutiques in the UK and Belgium.

Selected exhibitions
2006 *Origin*, Chelsea Crafts Fair, London
2006 Solo exhibition, as part of *Creative 8*, Clerkenwell Green Association, London

iris bodemer

Born 1970, Paderborn, Germany, lives and works in Pforzheim, Germany.
Having studied at Pforzheim's Academy of Design from 1992–1996, Iris Bodemer went on to further studies at both the Rhode Island School of Design in Providence, and the Sandberg Institute in Amsterdam. Her work is held in several public collections, including the Schmuckmuseum, Pforzheim, the Stedelijk Musuem in Amsterdam, and the Koch Collection in the Czech Republic. In 2001, she was awarded the Galerie Marzee Prize, and she continues to exhibit widely in Europe and the USA.

Selected exhibitions
2006 *bijoux, cailloux...*, Espace Solidor, Cagnes-sur-Mer, France
2005 *Hanging in Balance*, University of Texas, El Paso
2004 *Jewellery, the Choice of the Europarliament*, European Parliament, Brussels

silke fleischer

Born 1975, Biberach, Germany, lives and works in Antwerp.
Since graduating from Sint Lucas Karel de Grote Hogeschool in Antwerp in 2002, with a degree in Jewellery Design and Silversmithing, Fleischer has set up Silke & the Gallery, an open space in which she can present her work to larger audiences, beyond the conventional venues for the display of jewellery. She has exhibitied in a number of spaces beyond her own, and has also been lecturing in a number of visiting posts, including at Sint Lucas, and the Academy of Fine Arts, Sint Niklaas, since 2003. In 2004, she won an award from Friesfashion, B-Products, in Bruges.

Selected exhibitions
2006 *Somewhere In Between*, Sint Lucas, Antwerp
2005 *Fantasy Design*, Design Museum, Gand
2005 *Contemporary Women*, Espace Bizarre, Creative Lab/Lancôme, Brussels

Dongchun Lee

Born in Korea, lives and works in Seoul.
Having received a Bachelor of Fine Arts from Kookmin University, Seoul in 1992, Dongchun Lee moved to Germany to complete a Diploma in Jewellery, Hollow and Flatware in Pforzheim. Frequently shown in his native Korea, his work has also been recognised in exhibitions in the USA, Europe, and Japan, and he is represented by Galerie Marzee in Nijmegen, The Netherlands. It is also held in the collection of the National Museum of Contemporary Art, Gwacheon, Korea. He currently teaches at the Jewellery department at Kookmin University.

Selected exhibitions
2006 *100 Necklaces Filled with Dream*, The Collection Seoul Auction Gangnam, Seoul
2005 *Schmuck 2005*, Handwerksmesse, Munich
2004 *200 Rings*, Gallery Space, San Francisco

Carla Nuis

Born 1970, Barendrecht, The Netherlands, lives and works in Roelofarendsveen, The Netherlands.
Carla Nuis specialised in goldsmithing at the MTS Vakschool, Schoonhoven, The Netherlands from 1987–1991, before graduating in 1995 from the Academy of Visual Art, Maastricht. In 2005 Nuis completed a two-year Master of Philosophy by Project at the Royal College of Art in London, an institution where she frequently lectures. Nuis' many grants and awards include The Nicole Stober Memorial Award, Royal College of Art, 2005, as well as the Marzee Graduate Prize 2005, Gallery Marzee, Nijmegen, The Netherlands. Her work is in the permanent collections of The Contemporary Art Gallery, Laren, The Netherlands; Gallery Alternatives, Rome; Gallery Forum Ferlandina, Barcelona; and Charon Kransen Arts, New York, to name a few.

Selected exhibitions
2006 *Collect 2006*, The International Art Fair for Contemporary Objects, Victoria and Albert Museum, London
2006 *Schmuck 2006*, Museum of Arts and Design, New York
2006 *Two Close Ones*, Estonian Museum of Applied Art and Design, Tallinn

Lucy Sarneel

Born 1961, Maastricht, The Netherlands, lives and works in The Netherlands.
Lucy Sarneel began her tertiary education at Stadsacademie, Maastricht, 1982–1985, later continuing at Gerrit Rietveld Academie, Amsterdam, 1985–1989. From 2001 onwards, Sarneel has continuously shown her work through exhibitions across Europe, North America, Asia and Australia. Her jewellery has been purchased by nearly a dozen art institutions, including the Montreal Museum of Contempporary Art, Cooper Hewitt Museum, New York, Mint Museum, Charlotte, USA, The Netherlands Textile Museum, Tilburg, and the Stedilijk Museum, Amsterdam.

Selected exhibitions
2006 *Sterke Verhalen*, Stedelijk Museum, Amsterdam, and The Netherlands Cultural Centre, Erasmus Huis, Jakarta, Indonesia
2005 *10th Anniversary*, Gallery Funaki, Melbourne
2004 *Looking Over my Shoulder*, Lesley Craze Gallery, London

Karin Seufert

Born 1966, Mannheim, Germany, lives and works in Berlin.
Karin Seufert studied at the MTS Vakschool, Schoonhoven, and then at the Gerrit Rietveld Academie in Amsterdam. She has been exhibiting her work for over ten years, in galleries across Europe, in the US, and Tokyo, and her jewellery has been purchased by collections and museums in Tokyo and Arnhem. In 2004, she won first prize at the Frankfurt International Jewellery Competition.

Selected exhibitions
2006 *SOFA*, New York
2006 *Schmuck 2006*, Handwerksmesse, Munich and Museum of Arts and Design, New York
2005 *Fools Gold*, The Embassy, Edinburgh

Selected publications
500 Brooches, Asheville, NC: Lark Books, 2005
Op de Huid, Arnhem: Museum of Modern Art, 2000

Catherine Truman

Born 1957, Adelaide, where she currently lives and works.
Catherine Truman is a current partner of the Gray Street Workshop in Adelaide, which she co-founded in 1985, the same year as graduating from an Associate Diploma in Jewellery/Metalsmithing from the University of South Australia. Truman is an acclaimed jeweller who has exhibited and spoken extensively in Australia, Europe and the US; she has held residencies in the British School of Rome, and Manchester Metropolitan University, UK. In 1990 she studied Netsuke Carving in Tokyo. Her work is represented in over a dozen permanent collections, including the National Gallery of Australia, Canberra; Danner-Stiftung, Pinakothek der Moderne, Munich; and the Auckland War Memorial Museum, New Zealand. She is currently a Masters of Fine Art Candidate at Monash University, Melbourne.

Selected exhibitions
2005–2006 *Academici*, Monash University Art Gallery, Melbourne and British School Gallery, Rome
2005 *Transformations: The Language of Craft*, National Gallery of Australia, Canberra
2003–2004 *Light Black*, Jam Factory, Adelaide and Museum of Contemporary Art, Tokyo and Kyoto

Lisa Walker

Born 1967, Wellington, New Zealand, lives and works in Munich.
Lisa Walker studied Craft Design at Otego Polytechnic Art School, Dunedin, New Zealand, majoring in Jewellery, from 1988–1999. Most recently, Walker undertook studies at Munich Arts Academy, completing a diploma in 2005. Since 2004, Walker has collaborated extensively with celebrated artists and electro-pop trio, Chicks on Speed. She has received several academic scholarships and grants, including a Scholarship for Foreign Students through the Bavarian State Ministry of Science, Research and Art from 1996–2001 and the Creative New Zealand grant in 1995.

Selected exhibitions
2004 *Occidental Utopian Accident Part One and Two*, dual show with Chicks on Speed, Galerie Oona, Berlin
2003 *Glued, Bashed, Sewn, Squashed, Chucked, Painted, Soldered, Licked*, Jewelerswerk, Munich

annamaria zanella

Born 1966, Padova, Italy, where she currently lives and works.
Having studied Metals and Jewellery Design at the Pietro Selvatico Institute in Padova, 1980–1985, Annamaria Zanella went on to receive a degree in Sculpture from the Academy of Fine Arts, Venice, in 1992. Since then, she has gone on to receive a number of awards for her work, including the Herbert-Hofmann prize in 2006. She has lectured at Nuremberg's State Museum of Art and Design, and her work is held in a number of collections around Europe, and in the Museum of Arts and Design in New York.

Selected exhibitions
2006 *SOFA*, New York, represented by Charon Kransen Arts
2005 Solo exhibition, State Museum of Art and Design, Nuremberg
2005 *Annamaria Zanella and Salima Thakker Schmuckkunst*, Galerie Slavik, Vienna

LAYERS OF ADORNMENT

dinie besems

Born 1966, The Netherlands, lives and works in Amsterdam.
Dinie Besems studied at the Hoge School voor de Kunsten, Arnhem in 1987–1988, before moving to Amsterdam to attend the Gerrit Rietveld Academie, 1988–1992. Besems has work in the permanent collections of both the Stedelijk Museum of Contemporary Art in Amsterdam, and the Centraal Museum in Utrecht. Throughout Europe, she has been invited as a guest lecturer at leading institutions including Sint Lucas, Antwerp, the Royal College of Art, London, and the Design Academy Eindhoven, The Netherlands.

Selected exhibitions
2005 *Epibreren*, solo exhibition, Galerie Binnen, Amsterdam
2004 *Self*, Craftspace, Reizend, UK
2004 *Mannen, sieraden herenjassen*, Centraal Museum Utrecht, The Netherlands

monika brugger

Born 1958, Wehr, Germany, lives and works in Paimpont, France.
Monika Brugger began her studies at Pforzheim's Academy of Design and then Goldsmiths' school, going on to attend a number of prestigious institutions including the Academy of Fine Art in Antwerp and Edinburgh College of Art, eventually obtaining a Masters in Applied Arts from the Sorbonne, Paris. She has enjoyed a number of grants and awards, including an Artist's Residency at the Jakob-Bengel Foundation in Idar-Oberstein, Germany, in 2006. Her broad experience takes in curating, leading workshops, and speaking in conferences, beyond her work as a designer; the Schmuckmuseum in Pforzheim and the Fond National d'Art Contemporain, Paris, are among several institutions that hold her work.

Selected exhibitions
2007 *Métissages*, Museum of Fine Art, Bangkok
2007 *Au bout des doigts*, solo exhibition, Galerie V&V, Vienna
2006 *Collect 2006*, The International Art Fair for Contemporary Objects, Victoria and Albert Museum, London

madeleine furness

Born 1979, London, where she currently lives and works.
Having received a First Class Honours degree in Jewellery from Middlesex University in 2002, Madeleine Furness went on to undertake a Masterclass in 'Burned Jewellery' with Otto Künzli at the European Ceramic Work Centre in The Netherlands, and since 2006 has been mentored by artist Franko B, a training which has clearly impacted upon her interest in the relationship between body and object. She has lectured at various institutions and continues to be involved at Middlesex University as an Artist in Residence for the BA course in Jewellery.

Selected exhibitions
2005 *Art on the Borders of Art*, BWA Design, Wroclaw, Poland
2003 *Art on the Borders of Art*, Ex Canteri Navali, Venice
2003 *One Year On*, Crafts Council, Business Design Centre, London

Selected publications
Kulogowski, Yvonne, *The Earrings Book*, London: A&C Black, 2006

rheanna lingham

Born 1981, Maidstone, UK, lives and works in Snodland, UK.
Since completing her BA in Jewellery from Middlesex University in 2005, Rheanna Lingham has established her own business making fashion jewellery. As well as her training as a jeweller, she has experience working in millinery and leatherworking. Although she has only been working professionally as a jeweller for a relatively short time, she has already been exhibited in several galleries, and her work has been used in music promotions and photoshoots.

Selected exhibitions
2006 *Flight*, Stroud House Gallery, Stroud
2005 *International Graduation Show*, Galerie Marzee, Nijmegen, The Netherlands

husam el odeh

Born 1977, Saarlouis, Germany, lives and works in London.
Husam El Odeh studied fine art at UDK, Berlin, relocating to London in 1999 and completing a Bachelor of Fine Art in Painting through Chelsea College of Fine Art. While in London he undertook study in jewellery at Middlesex University, UK, graduating in 2005, setting up a studio and business the same year. In 2005 he was chosen by London's 'Fashioneast' to have a show during London Fashion Week and has since been sponsored twice by the esteemed British Fashion Council. El Odeh has collaborated with numerous fashion labels including Borba Margo and Siv Stoldals, and has his jewellery stocked in leading boutiques in London, Paris, Tokyo and Hong Kong.

Selected publications
2005 *Dazed & Confused*, UK
2005 *Another Man*, UK
2005 Italian *Vogue*
2005 *i-D* Magazine, UK

TIFFANY PARBS

Born in Nuriootpa, Australia, lives and works in Melbourne.
Tiffany Parbs completed an Advanced Diploma in Applied and Visual
Arts from the North Adelaide School of Art, majoring in Jewellery, in
1997. In 2000, Parbs was selected as an Artist in Residence with the
Silversmithing and Jewellery Department, Glasgow School of Art.
That year Parbs was also invited to be a guest speaker at Edinburgh
College of Art, and Adelaide School of Art. Over the past eight years
Parbs has been awarded numerous grants and accolades, as well as
having work featured on Australian television and in various
international books and publications.

Selected exhibitions
2006 *Cicely and Colin Rigg Design Award*, National Gallery of
Victoria, Melbourne
2006 *City of Hobart Prize*, Tasmanian Museum and Art Gallery, Hobart,
Australia

Selected publications
500 Bracelets, Asheville, NC: Lark Books, 2005
1000 Rings, Asheville, NC: Lark Books, 2004

SALIMA THAKKER

Born 1975, Wilrijk, Belgium, lives and works in Antwerp.
After specialising in Jewellery and Silversmithing for her BA degree in
Audiovisual and Fine Art at the Royal Academy of Fine Art in Antwerp,
Salima Thakker went on to take an MA in Goldsmithing, Silversmithing,
Metalwork and Jewellery at London's Royal College of Art in 2000; her
work has been shown regularly in exhibitions since she was a student. In
2002, she was awarded the Henry Van De Velde Award for Best Product.
She has designed collections for international jewellers Casa Damiani,
and currently teaches at the Royal Academy of Fine Art in Belgium.

Selected exhibitions
2006 Solo exhibition, Galerie Orféo, Luxembourg
2006 *SOFA*, New York
2005 Art and Craft Fair, Dubai

SMALL THINGS IN A WIDE WORLD

ROSEANNE BARTLEY

Born 1964, Auckland, lives and works in East Coburg, Victoria, Australia.
Having moved to Melbourne in 1989, Roseanne Bartley took a Bachelor
of Fine Art in Gold and Silversmithing from RMIT University in 1991;
in 2000 she returned to the University to begin a part time Masters.
Concurrently, until 2004, she was a tutor and course organiser at
NMIT in Melbourne for the Product Design and Jewellery course. She
continues to pursue academic avenues, but is also a working maker
whose jewellery has been shown around Australia and in the UK. Since
2003, she has sat on the committee of the Board of Craft, Victoria.

Selected exhibitions
2004 *Self*, Craftspace Touring, UK
2003 *Australians*, Perth Institute of Contemporary Art, Perth

Selected publications
"Culturing the Body", paper given at Jewellery and Metalsmiths Group of
Australia conference January 2006, www.craftculture.org

MACHTELD VAN JOOLINGEN

Born 1962, Niewkoop, The Netherlands, lives and works in Rotterdam.
Having studied at the MTS Vakschool, Schoonhoven in The Netherlands
and the Gerrit Rietveld Academie, Amsterdam, Machteld van Joolingen
has exhibited widely throughout Europe both in solo and group
exhibitions. His work is held at the Historic Museum in Rotterdam; in
2005 he won a WCC-Europe Award, and in 2006, he was given a project
grant by Artcentre Rotterdam.

Selected exhibitions
2006 *Maison et Objet*, Paris
2005 *Northern Fibre 6*, Kerava Art Museum, Finland
2002 *Cledinge*, Historic Museum, Rotterdam

TERESA MILHEIRO

Born 1969, Lisbon, where she currently lives and works.
Having studied to become a jeweller from 1987–1991, Teresa Milheiro
was a founder member of the ZDB Gallery in Lisbon in 1994. Alongside
this, she has worked for several years for the company Archeofactu,
designing jewellery inspired by Portugal's artistic and archaeological
heritage. In 2004 she was awarded a subsidy from the Foundation
Calouste Gulbenkian to develop a personal project, "Passage for One
Other Side", which is currently in process.

Selected exhibitions
2005 *Entrearte*, 9arte Gallery, Lisbon
2003 *Recycling*, Contacto Directo School, Rio de Janeiro

shari pierce

Born 1973, New York, lives and works in Munich.
Shari Pierce has studied for several years under Otto Künzli at the Academy of Fine Arts in Munich, having received her BFA in 1999 from East Carolina University. She has exhibited widely, both independently and in group exhibitions, across Europe and the USA. Her work is also held in the Galerie Marzee's permanent collection in Nijmegen, The Netherlands.

Selected exhibitions
2006 *Fronteras: Borders: Grenzen*, solo exhibition, Jewelers' Werk Galerie, Washington DC
2005 *Deconstruction/Reconstruction*, Gallery Sztuki, Legnica, Poland
2005 *Schmuck 2005*, Handwerksmesse, Munich

katja prins

Born 1970, Haarlem, Holland, lives and works in Amsterdam.
Educated at the MTS Vakschool, Schoonhoven from 1989–1993, and at the Gerrit Rietveld Academie in Amsterdam 1993–1997, Katja Prins has become an established and widely exhibited jeweller, having shown work all over Europe and the USA. Her work is held in a number of collections in her home country and around Europe, including at The Netherlands Textile Museum in Tilburg, the Glasmuseum Alter Hof Herding, Coesfeld-Lette, Germany, and the Amber Centre, Gdansk, Poland—a range of institutions that illustrates Prins' own diverse practice. She has also lectured in The Netherlands, Denmark, Sweden and Poland, at a range of institutions, and has won commissions both from private collectors and galleries.

Selected exhibitions
2007 Solo exhibition, Galerie Louise Smit, Amsterdam
2006 *Contemporary Jewellery, Metalwork and Textiles Inspired by Architectural Forms*, Lesley Craze Gallery, London
2005 *ALATYR 2005*, The Kaliningrad Amber Museum, Russia

Selected publications
25 Years of New Glass, New York: Corning Museum of Glass, 2006
500 Brooches, Asheville, NC: Lark Books, 2005

francis willemstijn

Born 1973, Hoorn, The Netherlands, lives and works in Amsterdam.
Francis Willemstijn began her studies at Hogeschool van Amsterdam in 1996, completing a degree in teaching in 2000, and going on to study at the prestigious Gerrit Rietveld Academie, Amsterdam from 1996–2000, obtaining a Bachelor of Fine Art degree. In 2004 Willemstijn set up an independent studio where she crafts her jewellery, as well as creating websites for other jewellery artists, and in 2006 was the recipient of the Stichting Funds Scholarship. Willemstijn continues to exhibit her work in galleries throughout Europe.

Selected exhibitions
2007 *Collect 2007*, The International Art Fair for Contemporary Objects, Victoria and Albert Museum, London
2006 *Heritage*, solo exhibition, Galerie Louise Smit, Amsterdam
2006 *Dutch Jewellery*, solo exhibition, Kunstcentrum Zaanstad, Zaandam
2006 *Koru 2*, South Karelia Museum, Lappeenranta, Finland

CAMEOS AND KEEPSAKES

melanie bilenker

Born 1978, Staten Island, New York, lives and works in Philadelphia.
In 2000, Melanie Bilenker received a BFA in Crafts, concentrating on jewellery and metalsmithing, from the University of the Arts, Philadelphia College of Art and Design, where she currently lectures. Among other accomplishments, Bilenker has been selected as a visiting artist in 2006 at Moore College of Art, Philadelphia, at Rhode Island School of Design, Providence in 2005 and at Millersville University, Millersville in 2000. Awards and honours include the Sienna Gallery Emerging Artist Award in 2003 and the Addie Grossman Annual Memorial Award in Jewellery Design and Creation in 2000, as well as work in the permanent collection of the Mint Museum of Craft and Design, Charlotte, North Carolina.

Selected exhibitions
2006 *Challenging the Chatelaine*, Designmuseo, Helsinki
2005–2006 *100 Brooches*, travelling group exhibition throughout North America
2004–2005 *200 Rings*, travelling group exhibition throughout North America

Selected publications
500 Brooches, Asheville, NC: Lark Books, 2005
1000 Rings, Asheville, NC: Lark Books, 2004

kim buck

Born 1957, Denmark, lives and works in Copenhagen.
Educated from 1983–1985 at The Danish College of Jewellery and Silversmithing, established, multi-award winning jeweller Kim Buck has owned and run a successful gallery and workshop in Copenhagen since 1989. From 1999–2001 Buck was a professor at the School of Design and Crafts, Jewellery Department, University of Gothenburg, Sweden; in 2004 he became a guest professor in the Department of Metal Design of the Konstfack in Stockholm, Sweden, and in 2006 he was teaching at Hiko Mizuno College of Jewellery in Tokyo. Currently Buck is a freelance designer for renowned Danish luxury goods company, Georg Jenson.

Selected exhibitions
2007 *Collect 2007*, The International Art Fair for Contemporary Objects, Victoria and Albert Museum, London
2005 *Signa Intima*, The Danish Museum of Art and Design, Denmark

lin cheung

Born 1971, Hampshire, UK, lives and works in London.
Maker and academic Lin Cheung graduated from the University of Brighton with a First Class BA in Wood, Metal, Ceramics and Plastics in 1994. She went on to complete a year's Jewellery and Silversmithing residency at the Bishopsland Educational Trust in South Oxfordshire, UK, followed by a Masters in Goldsmithing, Silversmithing, Metalwork and Jewellery in 1995–1997. She has been teaching since 1994, and is currently a visiting lecturer at the Bishopsland Educational Trust and Middlesex University. The recipient of numerous awards for her own work, including The Arts Foundation Award in 2001 and the Deloitte & Touche Award for Excellence in 1997, she is also a respected, published commentator on contemporary jewellery.

Selected exhibitions
2006 *Koru 2*, South Karelia Museum, Lappeenranta, Finland
2005 Solo exhibition, Gallery Deux Poissons, Tokyo
2005 *The Watkins Era: 21 Years of Innovation, Research and Style at the RCA*, Contemporary Applied Arts, London

Selected publications
Cheung, Lin, *Lin Cheung, jewellery and objects*, London: Photo ED Press, 2005
Watkins, David, *Design Sourcebook: Jewellery*, London: New Holland Publishers, 1999

cassandra chilton

Born 1974, Melbourne, Australia, where she currently lives and works.
A practising landscape architect as well as a jeweller, Chilton graduated with a Diploma of Engineering Technology (Jewellery) from Melbourne's NMIT in 2003, after initially training in Landscape Architecture at RMIT University, Melbourne. Currently completing a Bachelor of Fine Arts (Gold and Silversmithing), Chilton has lectured at the University of Melbourne's Faculty of Architecture and Design, and is an Associate at the Australian design practice Hassell. Cassandra has been the recipient of an Arts Victoria Grant for public sculpture in 2004 and winner of the prestigious Hobart Art Prize in 2006, among numerous other achievements.

Selected exhibitions
2006 Solo exhibition, Gallery Deux Poissons, Tokyo
2006 City Of Hobart Art Prize, Tasmanian Museum and Art Gallery
2005 *from a distance looks like flies*, Egetal, Melbourne

julia deville

Born 1982, Wellington, New Zealand, lives and works in Collingwood, Australia.
Since 2001, Julia deVille has been designing and making accessories under her own label, Abattoir. She holds a Diploma in Fashion Design from Victoria University in Wellington, and has qualifications in Gems and Gemmology, Gold and Silversmithing, and Footwear Design. She has been featured in a number of New Zealand and Australian media publications, and is a member of the Jewellers and Metalsmiths Group of Victoria, and of Craft Australia.

Selected exhibitions
2006 Cicely and Colin Rigg Contemporary Design Award, National Gallery of Victoria, Melbourne
2005 *Uncanny (the unnaturally strange)*, Artspace, Auckland, New Zealand

rory hooper

Born 1975, Jerusalem, where he currently lives and works.
Rory Hooper has been exhibiting internationally since graduating with a major in Jewellery and Accessories from the Bezalel Academy of Art and Design, Israel, in 2002 with a Bachelor of Fine Art Degree. Hooper is currently an independent craftsman and designer, as well as an instructor of metal raising, jewellery design and techniques with the Department of Jewellery and Accessories, Bezalel Academy of Art and Design. Hooper has been the recipient of the Sharrett Foundation prize in 2001 and 2003, and the Lockman Prize for Applied Design, Bezalel Academy of Art and Design, Jerusalem in 2002.

Selected exhibitions
2006 *Schmuck 2006*, Museum of Arts and Design, New York
2006 *The International Art Fair for Contemporary Objects*, presented by the British Crafts Council
2006 *Collect 2006*, The International Art Fair for Contemporary Objects, Victoria and Albert Museum, London

eija mustonen

Born 1961, Polvijavi, Finland, lives and works in Ylamaa, Finland.
Eija Mustonen has undertaken extensive studies in her native Finland, beginning with training as a stonesmith at The Craft College of Lappeenranta from 1981–1983, and continuing over the next four years at The Institute of Industrial Arts and Handicrafts in Lahti, majoring in Silversmithing. In 1997, after receiving more than a dozen grants and numerous awards, Mustonen completed a degree in teaching through The University of Jyvaskyla, Finland, spending time as an exchange student at Royal College of Art, London. Most recently Mustonen has completed an MA at the University of Industrial Arts in Helsinki, 2000–2006. A member of The Arts Council of Southeast Finland as well as the Arts Council for the Province of Kymi, Mustonen frequently exhibits throughout Europe and North America in solo and group exhibitions.

Selected exhibitions
2006 *Schmuck 2006*, Handwerksmesse, Munich
2003 *Hoytiainen*, solo exhibition, Gallery Atski, Helsinki, Finland, and Gallery Rantapaja, Lappeenranta, Finland.
2000 *SOFA*, New York and Chicago, represented by Charon Kransen Arts

julia turner

Born 1970, Madison, Wisconsin, USA, lives and works in San Francisco.
Julia Turner spent a year in Florence studying at the Lorenzo de Medici Institute in 1990–1991, before returning to the USA to take a Bachelor of Fine Arts from the University of Wisconsin in 1993, and a Master of Fine Arts from Miami University, Ohio, in 1995. Having lectured at the California College of the Arts in Oakland from 1995–1997, and at San Francisco State University from 1997–2003, she is now a member of the Faculty at the Revere Academy of Jewelry Arts in San Francisco. From 2000–2002 she was President of the Bay Area Metal Arts Guild. She continues to show her work at a number of galleries in the USA and beyond.

Selected exhibitions
2006 *Julia Turner: New Jewelry*, Velvet da Vinci Gallery, San Francisco
2005 *Contemporary Enamels*, Taboo Studio, San Diego
2004 *Schmuck 2004*, Handwerksmesse, Munich

Selected publications
500 Necklaces, Asheville, NC: Lark Books, 2006
"Observations: The Work of Julia Turner", *Metalsmith*, vol. 21, no. 1, Spring 2001

ACKNOWLEDGEMENTS

First and foremost, I am grateful to the talented and inspiring makers included in these pages, who have taken the time to provide images and information and allowed their work to be reproduced here. Lin Cheung is to be thanked in particular for her contribution – not only in supplying an insightful text that provides a way to negotiate the work presented, but in the sourcing of material to accompany her writing; she has been most generous with her time and wisdom. Beccy Clarke and Indigo Clarke have provided stimulating and well-informed texts for all of the makers, bringing to bear dedication, patience, and good cheer at every stage. Caroline Broadhead kindly stepped in to provide last-minute advice and an expert eye.

Oriana Fox deserves special mention as the commissioning editor of the book, overseeing the initial stages of research and the compiling of material. In assembling a body of work such as this, a tremendous amount of time and organisational skill is required. As the material piled up, co-editor Maisie Broadhead took on the unenviable task of sorting, selecting, and structuring with commitment and enthusiasm, bringing to the book a level of expertise and specialist knowledge that has enriched the process and the final product immeasurably.

Designer Emilia Gómez López has, as ever, approached a daunting mass of material with elegance and energy, to put together a design that makes a coherent whole of a disparate collection of work, while maintaining a sensitivity to the individual makers' approaches.

Amy Sackville

Profiles written by:

Beccy Clarke: Roseanne Bartley, Ela Bauer, Julie Blyfield, Sebastian Buescher, Julia DeVille, Silke Fleischer, Arthur Hash, Machteld van Joolingen, Dongchun Lee, Felieke van der Leest, Rheanna Lingham, Teresa Milheiro, Ted Noten, Katja Prins, Constanze Schreiber, Karin Seufert, Salima Thakker, Julia Turner, Annamaria Zanella.

Indigo Clarke: An Alleweireldt, Kirsten Bak, Dinie Besems, Melanie Bilenker, Kim Buck, Cassandra Chilton, Husam El Odeh, Karl Fritsch, Rory Hooper, Craig Isaac, Lindsey Mann, Marc Monzó, Eija Mustonen, Noa Nadir, Carla Nuis, Tiffany Parbs, Lucy Sarneel, Catherine Truman, Lisa Walker, Francis Willemstijn.

Amy Sackville and Maisie Broadhead: Iris Bodemer, Sigurd Bronger, Monika Brugger, Lin Cheung, Madeleine Furness, Shari Pierce.

Cover image: Installation: Francis Upritchard. Rings; Gold, silver, rubies, sapphires: Karl Fritsch. Earrings; Found materials, silver, gold, plastic: Lisa Walker. Photography: Daniel Mayer, www.danielmayer.com.
Section break images:
Natural Selection: Julie Blyfield, *Pressed desert plant* series brooches; 2005; Photography: Grant Hancock.
Playthings and Parodies: Noa Nadir, *frrrr* (detail); Ready-made clock, sewing machine parts, steel cable; 70 cm; 2002.
Artworks and Objects: An Alleweireldt, *Lollipop Brooch*; Lollipop sticks, waxed card, silver catch; 5 x 3 x 2.5 cm; 2006; Photography: EMS Photo.
Layers of Adornment: Rheanna Lingham, *Pigeon Wing Adornment*; Pigeon wing, ribbon; 2005.
Small Things in a Wide World: Roseanne Bartley, *Rosette*, brooch; Tin lid, 925 silver, enamel paint, stainless steel; 5 x 9.5 x 9.5 cm; 2006; Photography: Terence Bogue.
Cameos and Keepsakes: Cassandra Chilton, *Longhorn (Cerambycidae)*, brooch; Acrylic, 925 silver, stainless steel; 12.5 x 9.5 cm; 2005.
All photography by the artists unless stated.

Beccy Clarke
Holds a BA in History of Art from Goldsmiths College, London, and a First Class Masters in the same subject from the University of Edinburgh, completed in 2005. She also obtained a PG Cert with Distinction in Fashion and Lifestyle Journalism from the London College of Fashion, in 2006. She is now a freelance writer for *Dazed & Confused*, among other publications.
As a styling assistant, she works with photographer Neil Dawson, and has in the past worked with *The Scotland on Sunday's Fashion* magazine; she has also undertaken research for Rankin photography.

Indigo Clarke
Is a freelance journalist based in east London, where she covers all areas of fashion, music, art and design for leading magazines, including Australian titles *Oyster World* and *Russh*, as well as *Dazed & Confused*, UK. She completed a Bachelor of Arts Degree majoring in Art History and Theory and English at the University of Sydney in 2002, followed by postgraduate study at the University of Technology, Sydney, where she attained a Graduate Certificate of Journalism with Distinction in 2003.

architecture art design
fashion history photography
theory and things

www.bdpworld.com

Edited by Amy Sackville @ BDP and Maisie Broadhead
Designed by Emilia Gómez López @ BDP

Black Dog Publishing Limited
Unit 4.04 Tea Building
56 Shoreditch High Street
London
E1 6JJ

Tel: +44 (0)20 7613 1922
Fax: +44 (0)20 7613 1944
Email: info@bdp.demon.co.uk
www.bdpworld.com

ISBN 10: 1 904772 55 2
ISBN 13: 978 1 904772 55 2

British Library Cataloguing-in-Publication Data.
A CIP record for this book is available from the British Library.